T0135971

Markus Helfert
Regina Connolly (eds.)

Proceedings of the 1st International Conference on Business Innovation and Information Technology

Λογος

Bibliografische Information der Deutschen Nationalbibliothek

Die Deutsche Nationalbibliothek verzeichnet diese Publikation in der
Deutschen Nationalbibliografie; detaillierte bibliografische Daten sind
im Internet über http://dnb.d-nb.de abrufbar.

©Copyright Logos Verlag Berlin GmbH 2009
Alle Rechte vorbehalten.

ISBN 978-3-8325-2202-5

Logos Verlag Berlin GmbH
Comeniushof, Gubener Str. 47,
10243 Berlin
Tel.: +49 030 42 85 10 90
Fax: +49 030 42 85 10 92
INTERNET: http://www.logos-verlag.de

Proceedings of the 1st International Conference on Business Innovation and Information Technology

The 1st International Conference on Business Innovation and Information Technology was held in Dublin City University in January 2008 and focused on real-world business applications and innovations associated with information technology. Its purpose was to provide a premier forum for the presentation and discussion of business innovations associated with Information Technology (IT) and a platform for both researchers and practitioners to exchange knowledge and ideas and to learn from each other.

The conference had as its theme business innovation in what is an increasingly networked environment. Innovation involves the successful development and application of new forms of knowledge – new ideas, business practices, skills, and technologies – to create greater value for customers. It is critical to sustaining business competitiveness and in improving productivity. Improving innovation is therefore both complex and fundamental to the quality of our lives; it is also the foundation of our economic growth and jobs for our future. As a result, countries are developing national innovation strategies to enable them to become world leaders not only in the creation of knowledge, but also in the application of that knowledge in generating wealth, creating jobs, and promoting economic growth.

Innovation is also about removing obstacles, building a competitive environment for investment, and encouraging world-class business practice. Innovative strategies therefore focus on creating an environment that rewards well informed risk-taking and encourages businesses to invest in developing and commercialising new and improved products and services, implementing new and improved business processes, upgrading worker skills, and adopting new technologies. This conference brought together researchers and practitioners to discuss how that environment can best be developed and supported and in doing so to learn from the experience and reflections of others.

Many high quality research papers were submitted to the conference. The accepted papers were exceptional in terms of their originality, significance and contribution. It is hoped therefore that the papers contained herein provide the reader with new ways of thinking about business, processes, management techniques and systems of organisation – and in doing so act as a stimulus to the development of innovative approaches to business in the future.

Dr. Markus Helfert
Dr. Regina Connolly
March 2009

Table of Contents

INFORMATION QUALITY ISSUES HIGHLIGHTED BY DEMING'S FOURTEEN POINTS ON QUALITY MANAGEMENT

Mary Levis , Markus Helfert, Malcolm Brady
Dublin City University,
Ireland

Abstract. *In the last couple of decades the search for quality has been spearheaded by the Total Quality Management (TQM) philosophy, not only for avoiding failure and reducing costs but also for gaining competitive advantage. TQM is based on the principle that customers are the most important factor in the organization. There has therefore, been widespread interest in the practical value, of achieving International Standards Organization (ISO) levels of quality. These standards have commercial and economic significance for organizations. Professionals rely on data to successfully carry out their work and the quality of their information source impacts their decisions. However, good quality is hard to achieve and sustain. Ensuring information quality (IQ) is challenging, particularly in the healthcare sector, where they deal with large quantities of vital life saving information. Patients expect the healthcare service to be supported by effective high quality information systems so as to offer adequate service. Practitioners in healthcare are facing increasing complexities and a high rate of negative media coverage by failing to deliver a high quality healthcare service. Much of this can be traced back to IQ problems. However, Defining IQ has proved to be a difficult task and research in the field has not yet developed adequate theories, models and frameworks to address the issues involved. This study will primarily focus on Deming's 14 points to quality management as a means of identifying IQ problems in a healthcare delivery scenario. We will look at it from the perspective of those who use the data to carry out their tasks. Our study shows that while a variety of relevant attributes in a healthcare context can be assigned to many of Deming's 14 points on quality management we conclude that despite the fact that the basic tenets of quality are explained by leaders of quality such as Deming, Juran and Crosby, they are still not being forcefully followed.*

Keywords: Information Systems, Information Quality, Resistance to Change, EPR Systems, Quality Management, Total Quality Management.

1 Introduction

In recent decades the search for quality has been spearheaded by the Total Quality Management (TQM) philosophy, not only for avoiding failure and reducing costs but also for gaining competitive advantage. TQM is based on the principle that customers are the most important factor in the organization. Nowadays, there is widespread interest in achieving International Standards Organization (ISO) levels of quality. Over the last decade as healthcare has become more complex the diversity of services has become fragmented thus increasing the cost to the HSE without improving the quality of the healthcare system [1]. There is increasing evidence that problems encountered in the health service are not due to lack of funding, as expenditure in healthcare has increased considerably in the past ten years. According to a report in the 'Irish Medical Council', November, 2006, there was a €1.1 billion increase in health spending. Gross current spending increased to €13.9 billion. Total expenditure on healthcare in the US in 2004 estimated at $1.6 trillion [2]. In the UK, expenditure on its public funded National Health Service (NHS) is budgeted to rise to over £90 billion by 2007/08 [2]. Both of the Institute of Medicine (IOM) reports *'To Err Is Human'* [3] and the final report *'Crossing the Quality Chasm: A New Health System for the 21st Century'* [4] addressed a broad variety of quality issues when they alerted health care professionals to system defects and provided direction for significantly redesigning the health care system with IT playing a key role. They concluded that between 48,000 and 98,000 Americans die annually in hospitals as the result of medical errors, and this has necessitated radical changes in practice in order to eliminate errors and unnecessary deaths [3, 4, 5]. Many of these problems result from outdated, inadequate health care delivery systems that are not capable of providing consistent, high-quality care. Until the IOM report, however, medical errors did not receive the attention and awareness of the hefty financial burden to the health care system. Nevertheless, it is apparent that computerised information systems have not as yet achieved the same level of penetration in healthcare as in manufacturing and retail industries.

In Ireland many serious errors and adverse incidences occur in our healthcare system as a result of poor quality information (IQ). On a daily basis the media reports on the impact of poor quality in the healthcare sector [6,7,8,9,10,11,12,13,14]. Unquestionable evidence shows that the current systems in the Irish healthcare service are error prone and not delivering safe, high quality, efficient and cost effective healthcare [15], and for that reason is currently undergoing major reforms. A crucial factor of an effective and efficient healthcare service is information of high quality. Information is often not provided in the required quality [16]. Conversely, quality in a healthcare setting is a complex issue and can be accessed on two levels; the care provided by the information system and the care provided by the nurse. Juran states in his book 'the history of quality' *'what makes a difference to our modern world is our perspective of quality'* [17].

Yet, a universal definition of quality is difficult to achieve because nurses and patients define quality from different perspectives. To nurses, quality care could refer to how well they treat the patient. In contrast patients might place greater emphasis on bedside manner and at the end of the day patient satisfaction hinges on whether their hospital experience meets with their expectations. Consequently, assessing patient satisfaction and quality care depends on the perspective in which quality care is defined. For change to occur, healthcare professionals need to take the perspective of the patient into account. It is of critical importance to foster high-quality healthcare information to support high quality patient care at all levels of the healthcare system. This can be achieved by ensuring that good healthcare information becomes readily accessible and appropriately used in a quality rich professional manner. The measurements of performance should be tracked by employee, and by task, on a regular basis so that improvement of each employee can be plotted, and areas that hinder quality pinpointed and corrected. Following the policies of the hospital is critical for knowledge reuse in order to maintain the standard of care and to ensure high IQ in the knowledge base [18]. Quality assessment activities determine the extent to which actual practices are consistent with a particular indicator of quality, such as adherence to a practice guideline. We believe that many problems within the healthcare delivery service could be reduced if greater attention is paid to the quality of information communication, seeing that clear and precise communication is essential to providing high quality care.

Successful implementation of the Electronic Patient Record (EPR) is shaped by perceptions of changes it will bring to the performance of everyday jobs in the hospital. Many doctors dislike working with the EPR, and nurses frequently complain about having to be competent in their own profession and also having to have the skills to manage the turbulence caused by other professionals' resistance to using the EPR's which increases their workloads. More specifically, for an order-entry system, success in short, has many dimensions: effectiveness, efficiency, organizational attitudes and commitment, worker satisfaction, patient satisfaction—not all departments in the hospital may agree about which dimension is most relevant. There is a crucial need to shift the focus of research towards improving the capture; use; maintenance and transfer of high quality data to facilitate professionals in providing the highest quality healthcare possible. Everyone involved in the capture, use, transfer and documentation of healthcare data is responsible for its quality and ensuring the data is usable, accurate, comprehensive, consistent, relevant, and on time. Paper-based patient records have been in existence for centuries and their replacement by computer-based records has been slowly in progress in the last number of years. A recurring theme in literature is the effect of organization culture, which should have a strong positive effect on the process-driven / people-driven side of the business. The shift from traditional methods needs significant changes in skills, procedures, and culture that may require years to adjust. The traditional approach to quality however, predominantly focuses on technical aspects of quality and paying little attention to the soft systems (human side) of quality [19].

This paper argues that control of information quality is the responsibility of all stakeholders in the health service delivery chain. We will examine the impact of resistance to using the EPR system in a blood ordering scenario in a major Irish hospital. The rest of this paper is organized as follows: Section 2 traces the evolution of quality and its many definitions. Section 3: defines TQM; Section 4 briefly outlines IQM; Section 5 analyses of a case study mapped to Deming's 14 points on quality management; Section 6 gives a brief summary and conclusions.

3

2 Evolution of Quality

The roots of quality can be traced to the pre Industrial Revolution era, when inspection committees enforced rules for marking goods with a special quality mark to represent a craftsman's good reputation. 19th century manufacturing followed this approach until the Industrial Revolution. Late in the 19th century the United States adopted a new management approach developed by Frederick W. Taylor. Taylor's goal was to increase productivity by assigning inspectors, which led to a remarkable rises in productivity but, had a negative effect on quality. To remedy the quality decline, factory managers created inspection departments to keep defective products from reaching customers and quality was understood as conformance to standards [17, 20]. By the 1970's, the U.S. embraced approaches that involved the entire organization known as TQM [21], and since the turn of the century new management systems such as Information Quality Management (IQM) have evolved underpinned by the teachings of Deming and Juran [22]. Now quality has moved beyond manufacturing into service, healthcare, and other sectors [21]. But before quality can be managed, it must be defined. Quality has been defined widely in the literature as conformance to specification or fitness for use measured against some standard. However, the most widely used definitions are based on customer satisfaction and meeting or exceeding the customer's expectations. However, a universal definition of quality is difficult to achieve. Technically speaking, quality has two aspects 1 the characteristics of a product or service that satisfy customer's needs that are free from deficiencies; 2 the perception of quality from the perspective of those that benefit from the process, product or service [23]. Levis et al., outlines some commonly accepted definitions of the quality pioneers and their emphasis [24].

3 Total Quality Management

At the end of the eighties, quality became a crucial element in businesses all over America. To encourage international competitiveness, the Malcolm Baldrige National Quality Award was established in 1987. The birth of total quality came as a direct reaction to the quality revolution in Japan pioneered by the work of Deming, Juran, and Crosby [25, 26]. Rather than concentrating on inspection they focused on improving organizational processes [19, 27]. The focus in TQM is not on the technical aspect of service delivery, although technical skills are important. In essence, the three basic principles of TQM are: focus on customer satisfaction; seek continuous and long term improvement in all the organization's processes and outputs, and ensure full involvement of the entire work force in improving quality. TQM is always people-driven and its results are high performance team work, employee morale enhancement and a harmonious organizational climate [28]. However, the entire total quality effort must be planned and managed by the management team [29]. Most management leaders agree that the biggest ingredient and most critical issue in quality is management commitment [19, 30]. Management needs to make commitment to quality clear to the entire organization and communicate the fact that total quality continuous improvement is essential for success [28, 29, 30, 31]:

4 Information Quality

After an extensive review of the literature, an agreed definition of information quality also seems to be an elusive concept and difficult to define in a way that is conceptually satisfying [32, 33, 34]. There are a number of theoretical frameworks for understanding data quality. Levis et al. summarized the main points of some important models [24]. Redman, Orr and others present a cybernetic model of information quality that views organizations as made up of closely interacting feedback systems linking quality of information to its use, in a feedback cycle where the actions of each system are continuously modified by the actions, changes and outputs of other systems [19, 33, 35]. Data is of high quality 'if it is fit for its intended use' [36, 37, 38]. Wang and Strong propose a data quality framework that includes the categories of intrinsic data quality, accessibility data quality, contextual and representational data quality from the perspectives of those who used the information [39]. The goal of information quality management (IQM) introduced in the 1990's is to increase the value of high quality information assets [40]. Most researchers and practitioners agree, that the key to understanding information quality is to understand the processes that generate, use, and store data. However, quality cannot be measured in purely technical terms by some characteristics of the product or service. High quality Information is a critical enabler to TQM and, serves as a key to quality success. Better quality and productivity may not be the issue, but rather better information quality [41]. Information is critical to all functions and all functions need to be integrated by information. Organizational knowledge is based on exchange of information between customers, employees, information suppliers, and the public.

5 Analysis of Hospital Case Study

We will now examine what happened when the EPR system came to work as a fundamental part of the daily work practices in one of Ireland's major hospitals. A regular scenario was mapped from conversations and through in-person interviews with a staff nurse in one of Dublin's major hospitals. To disguise the identity of this hospital we shall refer to it as hospital H in this paper. Hospital H had just transferred from their outdated manual paper based blood ordering system to the new Electronic Patient Records (EPR) system. The EPR should become a valuable communication channel between doctors and other service departments. The implementation of this system should provide accurate and timely information and streamline work practices to increase information quality by reducing the inefficient manual paper based tasks. A description of TQM and how it maps to a hospital setting and the selected scenarios are tabled in appendix 1.

Scenario1: Dr 'A' attends to patient P in his out-patients consultation room in hospital H and decides patient P needs blood tests. He enters the blood order into the EPR and sends patient P to the Phlebotomy department. Patient P leaves the clinic and goes to the Phlebotomy department. The Phlebotomist checks the EPR system for the blood order for patient P. The blood order for patient P is on the system and therefore s/he proceeds to take the blood sample. The phlebotomist is highly impressed with the new system because of the instant communication channel and having no problems interpreting Dr A's handwriting. Fortunately, this new computer technology system has made it possible for Dr A to provide relevant information for the phlebotomist when they need it. This automated system improved overall efficiency and, thus, patient care quality.

Scenario 2: Dr 'B' also working in hospital H attends to Patient Q in his outpatients consultation room and decides patient Q needs blood tests. However, he feels that the implementation of the EPR system interferes with his traditional long standing practice of using the paper based blood ordering form and is reluctant to use the system. To him handwriting is mechanical—he does not have to think about it, but using the EPR system is not. He has concerns about spending too much time on the computer and less time with his patients. Therefore he fills in the outdated manual blood order form. Patient Q leaves his clinic and goes to the Phlebotomy department. The Phlebotomist checks the EPR for a blood order for patient Q. The blood order is **not** on the system. The Phlebotomist is not impressed as s/he does not have the appropriate information to carry out the task in hand and refuses to accept the paper form from Patient Q. The Phlebotomist insists that patient Q goes back to Dr 'B' to enter the blood order into the EPR. When patient Q arrives at Dr B's clinic, s/he is told that Dr B is attending to patient R. In order to pacify the irate patient the nurse on duty has to decipher Dr B's handwriting and enter the blood order details into the system herself before sending unhappy patient Q back to the Phlebotomy department. On the patient's arrival the Phlebotomist again checks the EPR for the blood order for patient Q and is happy to find it available on the system and proceeds to take the blood sample. Figure 1 show a typical high level process model to capture scenario 1 and scenario 2.

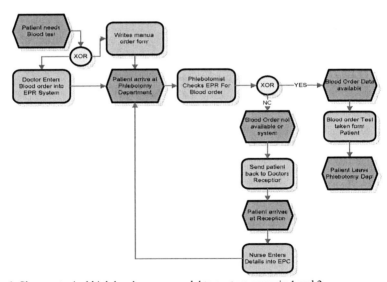

Fig. 1. Shows a typical high level process model to capture scenario 1 and 2

The ability to enter and store orders for blood tests, and other services in a computer-based system enhances legibility, reduces IQ problems, and improves the speed with which orders are executed. The automated record is highly legible, generally more accurate, and instantly available to the phlebotomist who normally had to struggle with deciphering all kinds of handwriting on paper based forms. The use of the EPR was strongly opposed by Dr B, which unintentionally slowed down the patient flow and adversely affected the nurse's workload just because it altered his traditional workflow pattern. Until the implementation of the EPR, doctors used to work with the paper based ordering system, which was easy to handle and did not take much time, whereas the EPR takes more time - a very scarce resource for doctors. Nurses however, because of their proximity to the patient have a key role in co-coordinating patient care and protecting them from all organizational turbulence. Technology changes information flows and because of this, it also changes relationships between health care professionals. Dr B's resistance to change is stirring up pre-existing conflicts with nurses and results in new confrontations between them. We conclude that this could be due largely to computer illiteracy or low level of IT expertise preventing Dr B from using the EPR. Table 2 and table 3 shows the above scenarios mapped to Deming's 14 points on Quality Management and figure 2 shows the processes mapped to some of Deming's 14 points.

Table 2. Scenarios 2 mapped to Deming's 14 points on Quality Management ✗ = Not Followed; ✓ Followed ✓✗ Followed / Not Followed.

	Deming's 14 Points on Quality	❶	❸	❹	❻	❼	❽
1	Constancy of purpose	✗	✗✓	✗	✗	✗	✓
2	Adopt new management philosophy	✗	✓✗	✗	✗	✗	✓
3	Understand the purpose of inspection						
4	Relationship between organization and supplier						
5	Continuous improvement of every process	✗	✓✗	✗	✗	✗	✓
6	Training and education	✗	✓		✗		
7	Leadership	✗	✓	✗	✗		
8	Job satisfaction		✓✗	✗	✗		✗
9	Barriers between departments	✓	✓✗	✓	✓	✓	✓
10	Slogans and targets						
11	Goals for management.				✗		
12	Pride in workmanship		✓	✗	✗	✗	✓
13	Training and education	✗	✓		✗		
14	Management transformation.		✓	✗	✗		

Table 3: Process mapped to Deming 14 points on Quality Management.

	Deming's 14 Points on Quality	Processes following the points
1	Constancy of purpose	❷ ❸ ❺ ❻ ❽
2	Adopt new management philosophy	❷ ❸ ❺ ❻ ❽
3	Understand the purpose of inspection	
4	Relationship between organization and supplier	
5	Continuous improvement of every process	❷ ❸ ❺ ❻
6	Training and education	❷ ❸ ❺ ❻
7	Leadership	❷ ❸ ❺ ❻
8	Job satisfaction	❷ ❸ ❺ ❻
9	Barriers between departments	❶ ❼ ❽
10	Slogans and targets	
11	Goals for management.	
12	Pride in workmanship	❷ ❸ ❺ ❻
13	Training and education	❷ ❸ ❺ ❻ ❽
14	Management transformation.	

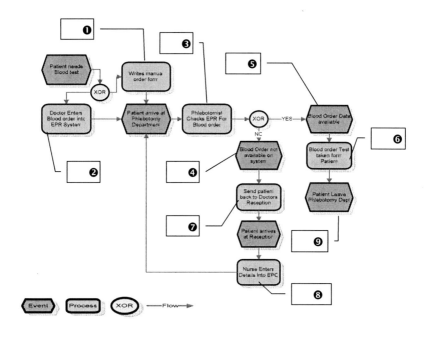

Fig. 2. Processes Mapped to some of Deming's 14 points on quality management

❶ Dr writes manual blood order here we see barriers between departments; ❷ Dr enters blood order into EPR points out adequate training and education; ❸ Phlebotomist checks for blood order on EPR highlights adopting a new philosophy; ❹ Blood order not available on EPR indicates barriers between departments; ❺ Blood order available on EPR signifies job satisfaction; ❻ Blood test taken form patient signifies consistency of purpose for improvement of quality for patients; ❼ patient sent back to Dr clinic indicates barriers between departments; ❽ nurse enters blood order into EPR suggests lack of training and education for the doctor and barriers between departments; ❾ patient leaves phlebotomy department happy would suggest management transformation and consistency of purpose for improvement of quality.

6 Conclusion

A major re-engineering of the health care delivery system is needed for significant progress to be made, which will require changes in cultural, educational and training factors. The heightened pace of modern practice dictates the use of EPR's, to improve quality of care and to build a safer quality healthcare environment. Yet, despite indication that clinical information systems can improve patient care, they have not been successfully implemented at least in Hospital X. Doctor B is still unwilling to change his long-established practice patterns of using the paper based blood ordering forms even though, automated records are highly legible, generally more accurate, instantly available and of higher quality for the phlebotomy department.

Our research shows that in hospital X resistance to change is an ongoing problem that hinders painstaking efforts to improve performance and quality and is seen as a major failure factor in implementing the EPR system successfully. Even though the benefits of the system are known, many individuals still need greater evidence to convince them to adapt it. One major obstacle is the time it takes physicians to learn how to use the system in their daily routine. Replacing paper based systems with EPR changes the doctor's traditional work practice; the relationships between doctors and nurses, and the work distribution. In our case study in hospital X there is a delay in accessing patient B's blood order and therefore the productivity of the nurse on duty was reduced and her work load increased. It also led to dissatisfaction among system users i.e. the phlebotomist, and patient Q as the end user of the healthcare system. Further research is needed to identify and assess other barriers to its use.

Management and human factors such as the information customer (the phlebotomist) and supplier (Dr 'A') played a critical role in implementing and maintaining a good quality healthcare system. Automating the manual tasks of blood ordering freed up paperwork time and increased the time spent with patient care. In scenario 2, Dr 'B' fell victim of some of the barriers to EPR, which can be identified as his a lack of IT skills, training and motivation. For Dr B, handwriting is second nature and he does not have to think about it, but using a computer is not. There is a need to change Dr 'B's' perception of the system, from seeing it as an additional burden to seeing it as a more effective use of time and as a way to improve patient satisfaction as the end user of the healthcare service. For change to occur a major re-engineering of the health care delivery system is needed. An effective total quality effort will require the participation of everybody in the hospital [28] and good communication with other departments is important to get richer information [29]. In a TQM effort, all members of an organization participate in improving the processes, services and culture in which they work.

As shown in scenario 2, attempts to computerize processes were met with strong user resistance. There are many different reasons for resistance for example psychological factors such as fear of change. Until the moment of the implementation of the EPR, doctors were used to working with the paper ordering system, which is easy to handle and does not take much time. With the EPR it takes much more time for doctors to order and time is a scarce resource for healthcare workers. The only cultural change necessary is accuracy and time needed to enter the order into the EPR once adequate training in using the system is put in place.

References

[1]   Fair Douglas C., Lighter Donald E,. Quality Management in Health Care: Principles and Methods, Jones and Bartlett (2004).

[2]   Irish Medical News, *'Mixed reactions to estimates, health estimates highlights'*, (2006)

[3]   Institute of Medicine,: To Err is Human: Building a Safer Health System. Washington, D.C.: National Academy Press (1999)

[4]   Institute of Medicine,: Crossing the Quality Chasm: A New Health System for the 21st Century. Washington, D.C.: *National Academy Press* (2001)

[5]   Berwick Donald M.: A user's Manual for the IOM's Quality Chasm' Report, *Hope project- the people to people health foundation, inc., Health Affairs* 80-90, (2002)

[6]   O' Regan Eilish, One in 10 patients is a victim of hospital blunders. In: *Irish Independent*, Wednesday 17th January (2007)

[7]   Walley Raymond, Our health-care is in meltdown. In: *Irish Independent*, Friday 19th January (2007)

[8]   Donnellan Eithne, 60% of A&E patients had errors in their prescriptions. In: *Irish Times,* Thursday 18th January (2007)

[9]   O' Regan Eilish, Quarter of patients 'unhappy with A&E'. In: *Irish Independent,* Friday 19th January (2007)

[10]   Mc Kenna Jean, Surgery cancelled for over 40,000 patients. In: *Irish Independent*, Wednesday 6th December (2007)

[11]   O'Meara Aileen, Deadly delays for cancer patients. In: *Irish Business Post*, Sunday 14th January (2006)

[12]   Keogh Elaine Mother died after ambulance went to wrong address. In: *Irish Independent*, Friday 15th December (2006)

[13]   O' Regan Eilish, Children find it hard to alert nurses for basic help. In: *Irish Independent*, Tuesday 28 November (2006)

[14]   Mc Bride Louise, Reports claim health workers systematically neglect children. In: *Sunday Business Post,* Sunday 26th November (2006)

[15]   O'Loughlin Ann, Hospital to blame for wrongful removal of man's Stomach. In: *Irish Independent,* Wednesday 6th December (2006)

[16]   Nadkarni Pravin,,: Delivering data on time: the Assurant Health Case Proceedings of the Eleventh International Conference on Information Quality Boston, November (ICIQ-06) 341-355. (2006)

[17]   Stephens, K.S., Juran J.M,: *American Society for Quality, (*2005)

[18]   Ghosh Biswadip, Scott Judy E., Capturing Knowledge Management in Healthcare and Technical Support Organisations, IEEE Transactions on Information Technology in Biomedicine, 162-168 (2005)

[19]   Beckford J.: Quality: Rutledge Taylor & Frances Group, London and New York (2005)

[20]   Fox, C., Frakes, W., The quality approach is it delivering, ACM, 25-29 (1997)

[21]   American society for quality http://www.asq.org

[22]   English L, TIQM Methodology, DM Review September (2003)

[23]   Endres Dr Al, Endres Al C,. Implementing Juran's Road Map for Quality Leadership: Benchmarks and Results, John Wiley and Sons, N.Y. (2000)

[24]   Levis, M., Brady, M., Helfert M., IQ Management: Review of an Evolving Research Area, 12th International Conference on Information Quality, 09-11 Nov 07, Cambridge, Massachusetts, USA (2007)

[25]   Deming, E. W,: Out of the Crisis, MIT press (1995)

[26]   Wheeler, S, Duggins, S., Improving software quality, ACM 300--309 (1998)

[27]   Dale B.G., Bunney H,: Managing Quality. Blackwell Publishing, (2003)

[28]   Omachonu, V, K. J. A. Swift, Joel E. Ross, Principles of Total Quality, CRC Press (2004)

[29]   Soin,: Total Quality Essentials: Using Quality Tools and Systems to Improve and Manage Your Business, Published McGraw-Hill Professional (1998)

[30]   Blades M,: Development of a simple model for analysis of quality. MCB University press (1995)

[31]   Crosby P.B.: Quality without Tears, The Art of Hassle Free Management, McGraw Hill Inc, New York (1995)

[32]   Wang R Y.,: A product perspective on Total Data Quality Management, Communications of the ACM 58--65 (1998)

[33]   Orr Ken, *Data Quality and Systems*, Communications of the ACM 66--71 (1998)

[34]   Stylianou A.C., Kumar R.L,: An integrative framework for IS Quality management, Communications of the ACM 99--104 (2000)

[35]   Redmond, T.C,: Improve Data Quality for Competitive Advantage, Sloan Management Review, 99—107 (1995)

[36]   Bugajski J, Grossman R.L., Tang Zhao,: An event based framework for improving information quality that integrates baseline models, casual models and formal models, IQIS 2005 *ACM* (2005)

[37]   Kumar G, Tayi, Ballou,: Examining data quality, Communications of the ACM, 54—57 (1998)

[38]   Olson J., E Data Quality: The Accuracy Dimension, *Morgan* Kaufmann, (2003)

[39]   Wang, R.Y. and Strong, D.M.: Beyond accuracy: what data quality means to data consumers, *Journal of Management Information Systems*, 5--34 (1996)

[40]   English L, The Essentials of Information Quality Management, *DM Review* September (2002)

[41]   Ross, J Elmore, Perry S,: Total Quality Management: Text, Cases and Readings, CRC Press, (1999)

Appendix 1. Deming's 14 points on quality management mapped to hospital setting.

.	14 Points	Hospital Scenario	Processes
1	Constancy of purpose	Management must demonstrate commitment to nurses and Doctors constantly.	2,3,5,6,8,9
2	Adopt new Management Philosophy	Doctors and nurses must learn or adapt to new technology. Nurses must seek never-ending improvement and refuse to accept any non-conformance from colleagues who resist change.	2,3,5,6,8,9
3	Understand purpose of inspection	Management must understand that the purpose of inspection should be to improve the process and reduce cost and communicate this to all staff	
4	Relationship between organization and supplier	The Hospital should not award doctors based on number of patient's seen- It has no meaning without quality. The goal is to have a single Doctor responsible for each order and develop a long-term loyalty and trust, among co-workers	2,3,5,6,9
5	Continuous improvement of every process	Management should take responsibility and become actively engaged in enhancing quality and productivity, continuously improving quality and lowering costs. The focus should be on preventing problems before they happen. By identifying resistance to change and dealing with it appropriately	2,3,5,6,9
6	Training & education	Training and education should apply at all levels of hospital staff.	2,3,5,6,9
7	Leadership	Management supports doctors in their leadership development and helps them to adapt to new businesses processes to achieve quality improvement.	2,3,5,6,9
8	Job satisfaction	Management must encourage effective communication and teamwork- all departments working in harmony using EPR, Unsatisfactory job performance may be due to lack of job security- fear of being replaced by the EPR, ignorance and misunderstanding of the job requirement to use EPR and poor supervision (hands on training).	2,3,5,6,9
9	Barriers between departments	Barriers exist at all levels of management, and within departments. (Resistance to change from old conventional ways of ordering bloods) Barriers also exist between the hospital nurses and doctors.	1,4,7,8,9
10	Slogans & targets	Slogans and targets leave the employee powerless to achieve the objective, constituted by management by fear, and should be eliminated. (Eliminate the source of fear of the non compliant doctor)	
11	Goals for management.	Goals should be set at a level that is achievable (giving the physician time to change over to new processes on a roll out basis and supporting them throughout the training period).	2,3,5,6,9
12	Pride in workmanship	Workmanship does exist in hospitals because doctors may not be aware of the Hospital's mission for improved quality and they are improperly trained, lack supervision and resources. Restoring pride of workmanship requires a long-term commitment by management. (rewarding doctors for compliance is important)	2,3,5,6,9
13	Training & education	Training and education should apply to all levels of the organization.	2,3,5,6,8,9
14	Management transformation	Complete management transformation and Total Quality	2,3,5,6,9

Modeling Data Quality in Information Chain

Mouzhi Ge, Markus Helfert
School of Computing, Dublin City University,
Dublin 9, Ireland
{Mouzhi.Ge, Markus.Helfert}@computing.dcu.ie

Abstract. Most information systems provide services through information chain, in which data are typically shared in multiple databases. The lack of controlling shared data usually causes data quality problems such as inaccurate and incomplete data. These data problems can generate social and economic impacts for example missing opportunities, losing customers and making incorrect decisions. In order to assess the quality of shared data, this paper proposes a model that mathematically evaluates data accuracy and completeness. Based on the assessment algorithms, we carry out a simulation in the scenario of information chain. The simulation results have shown that data accuracy and completeness are negatively related to time of using data and the error rate of data operations. Based on random selections of data operations, we can determine the correct time of using data and the optimal error rate of data operations. Additionally, in the identical refreshing period, accuracy decreases faster than completeness. This result provides the indications for data quality improvement.

Keywords: data quality, information chain, data accuracy, data completeness

1   Introduction

Most data and information quality research falls into two communities: database and management. Database community is technique oriented and usually uses the term "data quality", which is defined as the data that meet specifications or requirements (Kahn and Strong 1998). On the other hand, management community is business oriented and usually uses the term "information quality", which is defined as the information that is fitness for use by information consumers (Wang and Strong 1996). Although data and information quality have been used interchangeably in various literatures (Wang and Strong 1996, Strong et al. 1997, Kahn et al. 2002), to facilitate understanding, this paper uses data quality (DQ) to follow the database community.

Modern information systems typically include an information chain that distributes and shares data among entities of the chain. These shared data are respectively used for indented business operations of each entity, such as decision making and organizational management. At an interval time, data alignments are carried out to refresh the shared data among the entities. However during the interval time, data operations may be taken in the database of the entity. These data operations could generate DQ problems and impact DQ, in turn affect business performance. Therefore assessment and improvement of DQ are crucial in the information chain.

13

To assess DQ, Two major methodologies are proposed in literatures: one is task-independent and objectively assesses quality of raw data or component data (Batini and Scannapieco 2006, 7) in the database. For example, Oliveira et al. (2005) propose a set of rigorous quality rules to automatically detect DQ problems in databases. The other method is task-dependent and subjectively evaluates quality of information products in business environments. For instance, Lee et al. (2002) develop an AIMQ method to evaluate quality of information products and apply this method in five organizations. Recognizing the above two methods, Pipino et al. (2002) present an approach that combines objective and subjective assessments. Observing these assessment methods, most research focuses on assessing DQ in a single static database or DQ in information product inventory. Little research has been done to address DQ in dynamic processes or related storage entities.

Recognizing this issue above, the objective of this paper is to propose a model that can assess DQ in related databases and provide indications for DQ improvement in the information chain.

This paper is organized as follows: section 2 reviews the works related to this paper. Based on the review, section 3 proposes a model to assess DQ dimensions. Using this model, section 4 carries out a simulation in the scenario of supply chain. Finally section 5 concludes this paper by providing research findings and future works.

2 Related Research

Ballou and Pazer (1985) propose a model to assess DQ in multi-input and multi-output information systems. This pioneering work has addressed that output DQ is affected by input DQ and data processing procedure. According to "garbage in garbage out" principle, input DQ is directly related output DQ. However data processing can amplify input DQ, diminish input DQ or remain unchanged. Therefore their model is represented by Output DQ = Input DQ + Data Processing, where Input DQ and Data Processing are the functions of data values. This model is also confirmed by Ballou et al. (1998) in the environment of information manufacturing system. Ballou et al. state that output DQ is determined by both input DQ and processing effectiveness.

To further study DQ in data processing, Wand and Wang (1996) use ontology to assess DQ by addressing the discrepancy between information system and real-world system. They propose that DQ is determined by how well the real-world system is presented by information system. For example, incomplete DQ problems happen when the elements of real-world system should be presented but not presented in the information system. Thus DQ is the result of the relationship between real-world system and information system. It can be presented by DQ = f(RW, IS), where RW is real-world system and IS is the information system. In practical uses, the real-world system can be considered as referencing system.

To highlight the data operations on referencing system, Cappiello et al. (2003) propose a model to determine DQ in multi-channel information systems. The typical structure of multi-channel information system contains one referencing database and one operational database. Referencing database is used to refresh operational database for data alignment. In the database chain of multi-channel information system, one database is simultaneously used as operational database and considered as referencing database by another downstream operational database. During the data alignment period, referencing database may execute certain operations such as deleting or modifying data. These operations could result in low DQ in operational database since the corresponding data in its referencing database have been changed. Based on the well accepted DQ dimensions, Cappiello et al. focus on data currency, accuracy and completeness. They investigate how operations on referencing database affect the three DQ dimensions in operational database. In their model, Data currency and accuracy are affected by deleting and modifying data units in referencing database, and data completeness is affected by creating new data in referencing database. However in practical applications, data operations usually take place in both referencing database and operational database. Recognizing this limitation, our work attempts to assess DQ in operational database when both referencing database and operational database are operating data in the refreshing period.

By reviewing the three significant works above, we summarize their research foci and our research objective by the following figure:

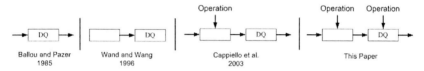

Fig. 1. Summary of literature review

From the figure above, we can observe that Ballou and Pazer (1985) focus on DQ in data flow among different data processing blocks. Wand and Wang (1996) concentrate on DQ which is determined by the relationships between referencing database and operational database. Cappiello et al. (2003) centre on DQ in the information chain, in which operational database DQ is influenced by operating referencing database. Extending these studies, our work investigates operational database DQ by considering data operations on both referencing database and operational database. Additionally we also provide indications for effective DQ improvement.

3   Model

A number of studies (e.g. Ballou and Pazer 1985, Wang and Strong 1996) have confirmed that DQ is a multi-dimensional concept. That means DQ is measured by a variety of dimensions, four of which can be objectively determined and frequently used in database community. They are accuracy, completeness, consistency and timeliness. In this paper, we focus on two most cited dimensions which are accuracy and completeness.

In order to assess DQ dimensions, we first need to map DQ dimensions to their DQ problems. To find out the related DQ problems, we need to determine which data operation generates what kind of DQ problems. This relationship is expressed by figure 2.

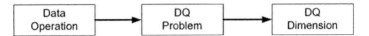

Fig. 2. Relationship between data operation, DQ problem and DQ dimension

As the figure above, data operations generate DQ problems, which then determine DQ dimensions. Using these DQ dimensions, this paper attempts to measure DQ in the environment of information chain. The typical feature of information chain is that different entities share data in their own databases and the shared data are periodically refreshed for data alignment. Consider DB_{m-1} and DB_m are the databases of adjacent entities in the information chain. In figure 3, DB_{m-1} and DB_m are respectively considered as referencing database and operational database.

Fig. 3. Typical information chain

As the referencing database, DB_{m-1} periodically refreshes the shared data in DB_m. during each refreshing period, data operations may be taken in both DB_{m-1} and DB_m. The typical data operations are create, update and delete. Following, we analyze the three data operations on adjacent databases during the refreshing period.

The data operation "create" means new data are introduced to the database during the refreshing period. If the data are only created in the operational database, there is no corresponding data in the referencing database. Therefore from the perspective of referencing database, data are redundantly created in the operational database. We term this operation as "Redundantly Create". If the same data are created in both operational database and referencing database or the corresponding data exist in the referencing database when we create new data in operational database, we term this operation as "Completely Create". If the data are only created in the referencing database, we term this operation as "Incompletely Create". In the above data operations, "Redundantly Create" generates redundant data problems and "Incompletely Create" generates missing data problems. Although "Completely Create" does not generate any data problem, it affects the total number of the data, in turn affects the value of DQ dimensions. The there forms of creating data in referencing database and operational database are described by figure 4.

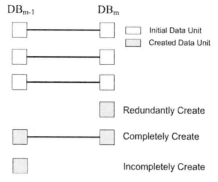

Fig. 4.   Data operation "create" in referencing database and operational database

The data operation "update" means the existing data in databases are modified during the refreshing period. After we modify the data only in referencing database, the corresponding data operational database is no longer consistent with the modified data in the referencing database. Therefore this operation makes the data in operational database incorrect. We term the operation as "Inconsistently Update". This operation consists of three situations: (1) data are only updated in operational database. (2) Data are only updated in referencing database. (3) The same data, in both operational and referencing database, are updated to different values. The three situations above all result in generating incorrect data in operational database. When we modify the data in both referencing database and operational database to the same value, no data relationship is affected by this operation. So we term this operation as "Completely Update". This operation does not affect any DQ dimension. The two forms of updating data in referencing database and operational database are described by figure 5.

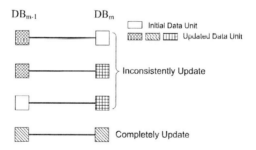

Fig. 5.   Data operation "update" in referencing database and operational database

The data operation "Delete" means the existing data in databases are deleted during the refreshing period. If we delete the data only in referencing database, no referencing data exist for the data in operational database. That means the data in operational database redundantly exist. We term this operation as "Redundantly

Delete". If we delete the corresponding data in both referencing database and operational database, we term this operation as "Completely Delete". This operation does not generate any data problem but influence DQ dimensions. When we delete the data only in operational database, this results in missing data problems and we term the operation as "Incompletely Delete". We describe the three forms of deleting data by figure 6.

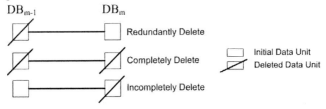

Fig. 6. Data operation "delete" in referencing database and operational database

From the discussion above, we can observe that data operations mainly cause three DQ problems: missing data, redundant data and incorrect data. Missing data exist when we incompletely create data in referencing database or delete data in operational database. Redundant data are the results of data which are redundantly created in operational database or deleted in referencing database. Incorrect data are generated by redundantly or incompletely updating data. Except the above data operations, although completely creating and deleting data do not generate any DQ problem, they still affect the value of DQ dimension because they influence the number of total data units. Therefore the only safe data operation is completely updating the data.

According to the definitions of DQ dimensions, we need to map DQ problems to data accuracy and completeness. Data accuracy is defined as data value conforms to the actual value (Ballou and Pazer 1985). Therefore the incorrect data, which inaccurately represent the actual value, are obviously mapped to data accuracy. The redundant data are usually inaccurately used since their referencing data cannot be found. That means from the user's perspective, these redundant data are incorrect. We, therefore, map redundant data to data accuracy. Data completeness is defined as the ability of an information system to represent every state of referencing system (Wand and Wang 1996). Accordingly data, which are missing to represent the data in referencing database, are mapped to data completeness. We summarize the mappings between data operations, DQ problems and DQ dimensions by figure 7.

Fig. 7. Mappings between data operations, DQ problems and DQ dimensions

To derive the functions of DQ dimensions, two assumptions are made: (1) users can access all the data in the database. This assumption is to highlight that we are able to access the data before we determine DQ dimensions since data accessibility is also a DQ dimension. It is also the premise for data operations. (2) Data in operational database become perfect after data alignment. In this paper, it is hypothesized that data in referencing database are considered to be a benchmark. Based on the two assumptions, we can derive the functions of accuracy and completeness. Firstly, we provide the major notations used in this paper (table 1).

Table 1. Notations of the paper

Variable	Symbol	Description
Database	DB_m	The database which is used in the mth entity.
Create	$C_m(t)$	This function is used to calculate the number of data created in DB_m at time t of one refresh period.
Redundantly Create	$RC_m(t)$	This function is used to calculate the number of data redundantly created in DB_m at time t of one refresh period.
Completely Create	$CC_m(t)$	This function is used to calculate the number of data completely created in DB_m at time t of one refresh period.
Incompletely Create	$IC_m(t)$	This function is used to calculate the number of data incompletely created in DB_m at time t of one refresh period.
Redundantly Update	$RU_m(t)$	This function is used to calculate the number of data redundantly updated in DB_m at time t of one refresh period.
Incompletely Update	$IU_m(t)$	This function is used to calculate the number of data incompletely updated in DB_m at time t of one refresh period.
Delete	$D_m(t)$	This function is used to calculate the number of data deleted in DB_m at time t of one refresh period.
Redundantly Delete	$RD_m(t)$	This function is used to calculate the number of data redundantly deleted in DB_m at time t of one refresh period.
Completely Delete	$CD_m(t)$	This function is used to calculate the number of data completely deleted in DB_m at time t of one refresh period.
Incompletely Delete	$ID_m(t)$	This function is used to calculate the number of data incompletely deleted in DB_m at time t of one refresh period.

Let's still consider DB_{m-1} and DB_m are the databases of two adjacent entities, in which DB_{m-1} is referencing database and DB_m is the operational database. Data are shared between DB_{m-1} and DB_m. The shared data set $DB_{m-1,m}$ can be expressed by:

$$DB_{m-1,m} = DB_{m-1} \bigcap DB_m \neq \phi \qquad (1)$$

In the information chain, the shared data in DB_m are aligned with DB_{m-1} every refreshing period. During the refreshing period, we determine data accuracy and completeness in operational database DB_m.

3.1   Data Accuracy

In the database community of DQ research, data accuracy is calculated by the ratio of the number of accurate data dividing the number of total data. That is:

$$\text{Accuracy} = \frac{\text{Number of Accurate Data}}{\text{Number of Total Data}} \qquad (2)$$

The number of accurate data can also be expressed as subtracting the number of inaccurate data from the number of total data. Therefore function 2 can be reformed to:

$$\text{Accuracy} = \frac{\text{Number of Total Data - Number of Inaccurate Data}}{\text{Number of Total Data}} \qquad (3)$$

In one refreshing period, the number of total data is determined by the number of initial data, deleted data and created data in DB_m. Specifically, at time t the number of total data is

$$N_t = |\, DB_{m-1,m}\,| - D_m(t) + C_m(t) \qquad (4)$$

Where N_t is the number of total data in DB_m. $|DB_{m-1,m}|$ is the cardinality of $DB_{m-1,m}$, which is the initial number of shared data in $DB_{m-1} \cap DB_m$. $D_m(t)$ is determined by $CD_m(t)$ and $ID_m(t)$ which both delete data in DB_m. $C_m(t)$ is determined by $RC_m(t)$ and $CC_m(t)$ which represent the data created in DB_m. Therefore,

$$D_m(t) = CD_m(t) + ID_m(t) \qquad (5)$$

$$C_m(t) = RC_m(t) + CC_m(t) \qquad (6)$$

$$N_t = |\, DB_{m-1,m}\,| - CD_m(t) - ID_m(t) + RC_m(t) + CC_m(t) \qquad (7)$$

According to the mapping between accuracy, DQ problems and data operation, inaccuracy is associated with redundant data and incorrect data, in turn, mapped to $RC_m(t)$, $RD_m(t)$, $RU_m(t)$ and $IU_m(t)$, which all generate redundant data or incorrect data. Therefore,

$$N_{ia} = RC_m(t) + RD_m(t) + RU_m(t) + IU_m(t) \qquad (8)$$

Where N_{ia} is the number of inaccurate data in DB_m. According to function 3, we can obtain:

$$\text{Accuracy} = \frac{N_t - N_i}{N_t} \qquad (9)$$

$$\text{Accuracy} = \frac{|\, DB_{m-1,m}\,| - CD_m(t) - ID_m(t) + CC_m(t) - RD_m(t) - RU_m(t) - IU_m(t)}{|\, DB_{m-1,m}\,| - CD_m(t) - ID_m(t) + RC_m(t) + CC_m(t)} \qquad (10)$$

In data operations, the combination of redundant operation and incomplete operation can appear to be the complete operation. For example, while we redundantly delete one data unit in DB_{m-1}, we also incompletely delete its corresponding data unit in DB_m. After the two operations, data are completely deleted and it is computed in $CD_m(t)$.

3.2   Data Completeness

Data completeness is calculated by the ratio of the number of data that represent the referencing data, dividing the number of total referencing data. That is:

$$\text{Completeness} = \frac{\text{Number of Data That Represent Referencing Data}}{\text{Number of Total Referencing Data}} \tag{11}$$

The data that represent the referencing data also can be expressed by subtracting the number of referencing data, which are not represented, from the number of total referencing data. That means subtracting the operational data that fail to represent their referencing data. Therefore function 10 can be reformed to:

$$\text{Completeness} = \frac{\text{Number of Total Referencing Data - Number of Missing Data}}{\text{Number of Total Referencing Data}} \tag{12}$$

In our case, the total number of referencing data is the number of shared data in DB_{m-1} at time t. which is determined by the number of initial data, deleted data and created data in DB_{m-1}.

$$N_r = |DB_{m-1}| - D_{m-1}(t) + C_{m-1}(t) \tag{13}$$

$$D_{m-1}(t) = RD_m(t) + CD_m(t) \tag{14}$$

$$C_{m-1}(t) = CC_m(t) + IC_m(t) \tag{15}$$

$$N_r = |DB_{m-1}| - RD_m(t) - CD_m(t) + CC_m(t) + IC_m(t) \tag{16}$$

Where N_r is the number of total referencing data in DB_{m-1}. $|DB_{m-1}|$ is the cardinality of DB_{m-1}, which is the initial number of shared data in DB_{m-1}. According to the mapping between completeness, DQ problems and data operations, we can observe that incompleteness is only related to $IC_m(t)$ and $ID_m(t)$. That indicates although the data in DB_m may not correctly represent the corresponding data in DB_{m-1}, they do not influence data completeness because they are still representing referencing data but in the incorrect way. Therefore

$$N_{ic} = IC_m(t) + ID_m(t) \tag{17}$$

Where N_{ic} is the number of data in DB_{m-1} without presentations in DB_m. According to function 12, we can obtain:

$$\text{Completeness} = \frac{N_r - N_{ic}}{N_r} \tag{18}$$

$$\text{Completeness} = \frac{|DB_{m-1}| - RD_m(t) - CD_m(t) + CC_m(t) - ID_m(t)}{|DB_{m-1}| - RD_m(t) - CD_m(t) + CC_m(t) + IC_m(t)} \tag{19}$$

In the assessment of accuracy and completeness, the functions of data operations are not determined by data operations executed before time t. It is at time t we assess the data alternations and link them to data operations, whereby the output of data operation functions can be calculated.

6   Conclusion

In this paper, we propose a model to assess DQ in the environment of information chain. The model consists of three major components: data operations, DQ problems and DQ dimensions. We focus three frequently used data operations: create, update and delete. In each operation, we divide the operation into redundant operation, complete operation and incomplete operation. During the refreshing time in information chain, these data operations may generate DQ problems. Based on the identification of DQ problems, we map these DQ problems to DQ dimensions. As DQ is multi-dimensional concept, we focus on two most cited DQ dimensions: accuracy and completeness. To further detail the model, accuracy is mapped to incorrect and redundant data problems, and completeness is mapped to miss data problems. Each problem is connected with different data operations. According to the relationship between data operations, DQ problems and DQ dimensions, we propose algorithms to determine data accuracy and completeness. Using the algorithms, it is able to determine data accuracy and completeness in the dynamic environment of information chain.

Once the algorithms of accuracy and completeness have been determined, two possible extensions of this paper can be addressed. First, more DQ dimensions need to be involved in the model such as timeliness and consistency. When more dimensions are considered in the model, different dimensions may share the same DQ problems. That means DQ dimensions may be dependent on each other. Therefore considering the cost of fixing DQ problems, it is possible to find the optimal cost to improve the DQ. Second, when we consider the costs of poor DQ and costs improving DQ, it is also possible to find an effective strategy for DQ improvement in the information chain management.

References

1. Ballou, D. P., Pazer, H. L.: Modeling Data and Process Quality in Multi-input, Multi-output Information Systems. Management Science, Vol. 31, No. 2, pp. 150-162. (1985)
2. Ballou, D. P., Wang R. Y., H. Pazer, Tayi G. K.: Modeling Information Manufacturing Systems to Determine Information Product Quality. Management Science, Vol. 44, No. 4, pp. 462-484. (1998)
3. Batini C., Scannapieco M.: Data Quality, Concepts, Methodologies and Techniques, Springer. (2006)
4. Cappiello C., Francalanci C., Pernici B: Time-Related Factors of Data Quality in Multichannel Information Systems, Journal of Management Information Systems, Vol. 20 No. 3, pp. 71-91. (2004)
5. Kahn B., Strong D., Wang R.Y.: Information Quality Benchmarks: Product and Service Performance, Communications of the ACM, Vol. 45 No. 4, pp. 184-192. (2002)

6. Lee Y., Strong D., Kahn B., Wang R. Y.: AIMQ: A Methodology for Information Quality Assessment, Information & Management, Vol. 40, No. 2, pp. 133-146. (2002)
7. Oliveira P., Rodrigues F., Henriques P.: A Formal Definition of Data Quality Problems, Proceedings of the 10th International Conference on Information Quality. (2005)
8. Pipino L., Lee Y.W., Wang R.Y.: Data Quality Assessment, Communications of the ACM. pp. 211-218. (2002)
9. Strong D., Lee Y., and Wang R. Y. Data Quality in Context, Communications of the ACM, Vol. 40 No. 5, pp. 103-110. (1997)
10. Wand Y. and Wang R. Y.: Anchoring data quality dimensions in ontological foundations, Communications of the ACM, Vol.39 No.11, pp.86-95. (1996)
11. Wang, R. Y., Strong, D. M. Beyond accuracy: What Data Quality Means to Data Consumers. Journal of Management Information System, Vol. 12 No. 4, pp. 5-34. (1996)

Business Model Driven Service Architecture Design for Enterprise Application Integration

Veronica Gacitua-Decar and Claus Pahl

School of Computing, Dublin City University, Dublin 9, Ireland.
vgacitua|cpahl@computing.dcu.ie

Abstract. Organisations are increasingly using Service-Oriented Architecture (SOA) as an approach to create solution for Enterprise Application Integration (EAI) and business process automation. In this paper we present an architecture development process supported by business reference models and patterns. The process guides the transition from business models to a service-based software architecture solution. Firstly, business processes models are enhanced with domain model elements, application architecture elements and business-level patterns. Afterwards, business reference models and patterns are exploited to identify software services and their dependencies. The subsequent activities are focused on the transformation of the enhanced business process model to a service-based architecture that solves the application integration problem.

Key words: Service oriented architecture, enterprise application integration, reference model, business pattern, SOA pattern.

1 Introduction

Business Process Management (BPM) aims to improve the productivity, product quality, and operations of an enterprise [1]. BPM encompasses methods, techniques, and tools to support the analysis, design, implementation and governance of operational business processes [2]. Software applications are built or acquired to provide specialised functionality required by business processes. If new activities and applications are created and integrated into existing business processes and infrastructures, new architecture and information requirements need to be satisfied. Enterprise Application Integration (EAI) aims to link separate applications into an integrated system supporting the operation of business processes [3]. Increasingly, enterprises are using Service-Oriented Architectures (SOA) as an approach to EAI [4]. SOA has the potential to bridge the gap between business and technology, improve reuse of existing applications and interoperability with new ones. Software services are the building blocks for SOA, and they can be composed to provide a more coarse grained functionality and to automate business processes [5]. However, if new applications are often created without a structured architectural design, integrating these into a coherent architecture closely aligned with the business domain becomes a significant challenge. On top of specific architectures, architecture abstractions such as reference models, patterns, and styles have been used to allow reuse of successfully applied architectural designs, improving the quality of software [6, ?]. The continual rise of abstraction in software engineering approaches is a central driver of this work, placing the notion of patterns at business domain and focusing on its subsequent transformation to a software architecture.

The main contribution of this paper is a software architecture approach that provides a tractable and consistent transition from business models to software service architectures.

- The architecture approach is structured in layers. They separate aspects and beneficiates the maintainability of the architecture. Explicit connections between elements of different layers provide advantageous traceability characteristics, essential for change management. A modelling technique capturing the layered architecture provides coherence between business models and the software architecture. Standardised notation at business and software level [7, 8] promotes a broad use of the approach.
- Three core activities are performed along the proposed architecture development process: modelling, identification and transformation. Several steps from these activities have the potential to be automated. Automation encourages reduction of the human errors and an increase in the quality of products.
- The proposed process is distinguished by exploiting architecture abstractions -reference models and patterns- to identify software services and their dependencies. A derived advantage of incorporating architecture abstractions is the positive contribution over the maintainability of the architecture. Patterns are separated abstractions from specific architectures and remain valid as long as no large changes occur at business and application levels. Our approach is independent of commercial infrastructure. Large software providers might offer support to design service-centric solutions based on their own reference architectures, often dependant on technology.

This article is structured as follow. Firstly, a layered architecture structuring the application integration problem and the required architectural concepts are presented in section 2. Section 3 introduces a case study and explains the architecture development process. Section 4 discusses our approach. Related work and conclusions are presented in sections 5 and 6 respectively.

2 Layered Architecture

A *software architecture* explains the design of a system, describing each element of the design, their organisation, allocation and collaboration. It also characterizes the behaviour of the system [9]. Architecture abstractions are separate architecture descriptions independent of specific designs that posses some characteristic features. They constrain design elements and their relations, and in the case of patterns, they define solutions to specific design problems.

In this paper we propose a layered architecture structuring an application integration problem. The approach uses architectural abstractions to support

25

the incremental transformation from models at business level to a service architecture solution. The Fig. 1 depicts the considered architecture layers, their elements and architecture abstractions. Note that modelling of business processes and domain concepts is a previous activity, out of the scope of this proposal. Similarly, the implementation of services is a post-activity to the proposed process for designing service architecture solution for EAI.

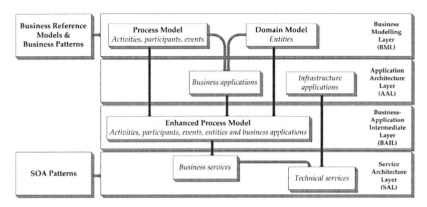

Fig. 1. Layered architecture structuring the EAI problem.

2.1 Architecture Abstractions

Business Reference Models. According to [9], a reference model is a standard decomposition of a known problem into parts that cooperatively solve the problem. Reference models arise from experience, and together with architectural patterns, they can constitute reference architectures. A *business reference model* is a standard decomposition of a specific business domain, often provided by standardisation organisations.

Business and SOA Patterns. Patterns have been broadly adopted as a medium to reuse architectural design knowledge and improve quality of software [6, ?]. Design patterns [6] are considered as micro-architectures solving recurring design problems contributing to the overall system architecture. *SOA patterns* solve design problems in the context of service oriented architectures.

Some influential efforts such as [10] focus on patterns as abstractions capturing and describing business modelling problems and their corresponding solutions so that they can be reused. Similarly to the work presented in [10] and [6], we consider *business patterns* as micro-models solving reoccurring business modelling problems. They can be reused and contribute to the overall business model in a specific domain.

2.2 Layers

The proposed layered architecture is composed of three main layers: the Business Modelling Layer (BML), the Application Architecture Layer (AAL) and the Service Architecture Layer (SAL). An intermediate layer containing enhanced process models provide an integrated view of BML and AAL. Layers separate aspects of the integration problem, thus contributing to the architecture maintainability [9]. Explicit connections between elements in different layers provides beneficial traceability characteristics, essential for change management.

Business Modelling Layer (BML). BML constrains and drives the integration of software applications. It has two main models: the business process model and the domain model. While business process models capture the dynamics of the business, domain models capture structural relations between business concepts. We have adopted the Business Process Modelling Notation (BPMN) [7] as notational basis for business models and their transformation to a service architecture. BPMN has been incrementally adopted over the last few years to model processes at business levels. We have also adopted UML 2.0 class diagrams [8] for domain modelling. They are suitability to our approach and facilitate the integration of BML and AAL.

Application Architecture Layer (AAL). This layer constitutes the technical scenario of the application integration problem and acts as architectural constrain to define technical services and their composition. AAL has both an inter- and an intra- organizational scope, since the business processes involved in the EAI problem can span across organizations. In order to define applications in architectural terms -and services in SAL- we borrow the component and connector view from [11]. This view defines a system as a set of components, where each component has a set of ports with interfaces. Interfaces enables the interaction with other components through connectors. We have consider the UML 2.0 component diagrams [8] notation for models in this layer.

Business-Application Intermediate Layer (BAIL). In this layer, process models are enhanced with elements of the domain model and applications. The creation of BAIL models is the first step towards the development of the service architecture. The notation used here is inherited from the previous layers.

Service Architecture Layer (SAL). SAL is the layer containing the services of EAI solution and it is structured as a service architecture. Software services are software components capable of performing a set of offered tasks. Services might delegate their responsibility of performing tasks to other services or software applications. Services can be composed to provide a more coarse grained functionality and to support the integration of processes. In this paper we discriminate between business and technical services. Business services abstract activities or business entities from BML into SAL. Technical services abstract functionality and data provided by AAL into SAL, as well as, functionality required to manage technical issues such as security, messaging, etc. We adopt UML 2.0 components diagrams [8] to represent services and their connections.

3 Layered Architecture Development Process

This section explains the proposed development process to design service-centric architecture solution for EAI trough a case study.

3.1 Case Study

The case study involves a *billing and payment process* representing a typical process where customers and businesses interact. The Fig. 2 illustrates a high level view of the process. Three participants (roles) are exhibited at this level, *customer*, *banks network* and *utility company*. The process indicates that an utility company is periodically billing their customers. A customer receive his invoice and decides to pay his bill or accumulate it as a debt. Note that for the sake of simplicity this example shows only a bank transfer as a medium of payment. After the payment transaction is completed, the bank's network sends the remittance information to the customer and the biller.

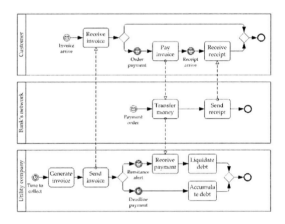

Fig. 2. Billing and payment process modelled with the BPMN notation.

3.2 Description of Development Activities

The main activities of the development process are: *modelling, identification* and *transformation. Modelling* activities enhance models from one layer adding new elements and relations -trace links- to models in the same layer or models in other layers. *Identification* activities are performed to identify business and technical services; and also to identify suitable business reference models and patterns. *Transformation* activities apply a set of rules to transform an original model in a new model that incorporates components emerged during the identification activities.

3.3 Development Process

The presented development process is a systematic approach to design service-centric solutions for EAI. The process consists of a set of activities structuring information from the business and IT sides of an enterprise. External information from the business and software community is also added in the form of business reference models and patterns. The Fig.3 depicts the development process. The participants of this process can be related to common roles in the IT industry. Business analysts or enterprise architects are suitable for modelling and identification activities at BML, BAIL and SAL. Software architects are suitable for activities at AAL, BAIL and SAL.

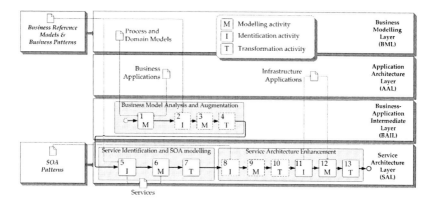

Fig. 3. Layered architecture development process

Business Model Analysis and Augmentation

Step 1. At the beginning of the development process, trace links between business process models in BML, domain model elements in BML and business applications in AAL are modelled. It creates an enhanced process model at the BAIL layer. The enhancement process starts decomposing the high level process model in BML until reach atomic activities. Trace links to domain model elements related to the data flowing through atomic activities are created. Trace links to application components manipulating the traced domain elements are also added. The Fig. 4 illustrates, as an example, the enhanced *generate invoice* activity (first activity performed by the utility company in the Fig. 2).

Step 2. This step involves the identification of an appropriate business reference model and associated business patterns. They facilitate the recognition of reusable sections of the business model, setting boundaries to define reusable business services and supporting the early identification of dependencies between services. We have selected the Electronic Bill Presentment and Payment

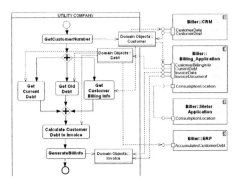

Fig. 4. Generate invoice activity with elements of the domain model and applications.

(EBPP) reference model for the case study. This reference model have been published by NACHA [12], an organisation representing more than 11,000 financial institutions. After analysing the process model we found that one of the process participants was playing the role of *mediator*. This role is also found in the *mediator pattern* [6], which aim is to solve a many to many communication problem. Specifically, we identify a *customer service provider* mediating between many customers and utility companies. The relation is illustrated in the Fig. 5.

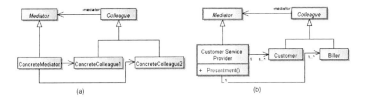

Fig. 5. (a) The *mediator pattern* from [6] and (b) its analogous at business level.

Step 3-4. These two steps involve modelling and transformation activities. They are performed to transform original BML models into enhanced models including elements and relations from business patterns. The Fig. 6 shows an example where elements and relations from the *mediator pattern* were incorporated to the original business domain model. The *Customer Service Provider*, *Mediator* and *Colleague* elements from Fig. 5 were added to the original domain model.

Service Identification and SOA Modelling

Step 5. In this step services are identified. Service design principles [4] such as loose coupling, abstraction, reusability and autonomy are considered. For the case study, and based on established processes from the EBPP reference model, the *bill creation, presentment* and *payment* composite activities were considered to constitute business services. Since *customer* is a central concept to these activities, we also identify this element as a data-centric. The *customer* service

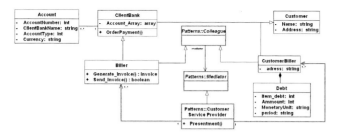

Fig. 6. Extract of the enhanced billing and payment domain model.

abstracts the customer information from different data sources in the biller side. The data sources encompass a customer relationship management (CRM) application; an enterprise resource planning (ERP) application; and two custom built applications, the *billing* and *metering* applications. The *transfer money* activity in Fig. 2 is further decomposed into three activities, the *initial payment* (customer side); the *clearing*, performed to manage taxes and other charges related to transactions between financial institutions; and the final *settlement* activity. Based on the latter, we define three more fined grained services composing the *payment* service, i.e. the *pay* service, the *clearing* service and the *settlement* service. Two technical services, *tariff* and *meter* services, were derived to abstract the tariff rules embedded into the ERP application, and the information regarding customer consumption managed in the *meter* application.

Step 6. This step incorporates the services identified in the previous step into the enhanced process model. An example is shown in the Fig. 7, where services and their dependencies are added into the model from Fig. 4. Note that service dependencies reduce the space of possibilities for service composition to the context provided by models in BAIL.

Step 7. In this activity the enhanced process model with identified services is transformed into a software architecture. Firstly, the dependencies between BML and AAL elements are hidden. Subsequently, the elements from BML are also hidden. The Fig. 8 illustrate the resultant software architecture after the transformation of the process model from Fig. 7.

Service Architecture Enhancement

Step 8-10. These three steps focus on the identification and incorporation of applicable SOA patterns. When implementing a service architecture, specific components supporting technical aspects such as service invoking, composition, security, among others functionalities are required. After identifying suitable SOA patterns, elements from those patterns are actually modelled into the service architecture. Transformation activities provide consistency to the final architecture. For instance, in the case study, services on the biller side could follow the schema proposed by the enterprise service bus (ESB) pattern [13]. By using this

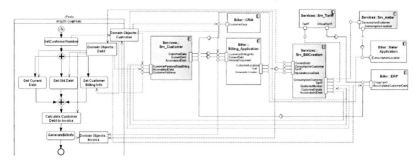

Fig. 7. Generate bill activity with elements of the domain model, applications and services.

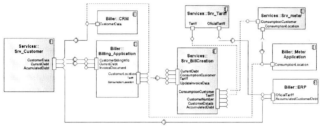

Fig. 8. Software architecture with services and applications.

pattern software components are exposed and managed through a centralized component that handles communication between services and their underlying legacy application support.

Step 11. In order to design a concrete solution to the previously incorporated SOA patterns, the identification of concrete software infrastructure is required. For instance, the ESB pattern mentioned in the previous step could be implemented with a specific commercial ESB infrastructure.

Step 12. At this stage, the identified infrastructure in the previous step and the required connections are modelled into the AAL. The Fig. 9a shows the new added component (ESB) into the architecture from Fig. 8. Note that redundant relations could appear after the inclusion of new infrastructure elements.

Step 13. The last step of the development process generates a service-centric architecture where redundant relations appeared in the previous activity are hidden. The Fig. 9b shows the architecture solution after hiding redundant relations.

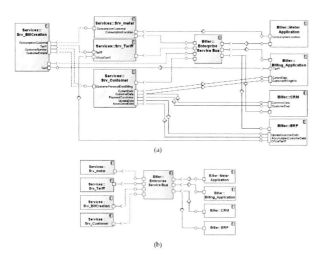

(a)

(b)

Fig. 9. Final service-centric architecture solution, before (a) and after (b) hiding redundant relations.

4 Discussion

Service-centric architectures have received considerable attention over the last few years. However, the focus has been mainly on improving technological infrastructure and run-time issues [14]. Design-time aspects have received less consideration. Practical experiences indicate that successful implementations of service design solutions in enterprises require systematic approaches to design architectures aligned to the business levels and with improved maintainability characteristics [4]. In this paper we have presented an architectural approach to design service-centric solutions for EAI. Coherence between business levels and the software architecture solution is provided through a consistent modelling framework and a systematic process that was demonstrated through a case study. Potential automation of activities in the development process was illustrated by a structured and guided step by step process. Maintainability of the architecture solution is beneficed by the explicit modelled trace links between elements in different layers of the proposed architecture. In order to evaluate modifiability, the Architecture-Level Modifiability Analysis (ALMA) [15] can be used. The ALMA method consider a change scenario elicitation, evaluation and interpretation. Possible change scenarios includes changes in business processes, domain models and the enterprise application architecture. Changes in process and domain models affect the BAIL layer, and the analysis of their consequences to the architecture solution can be facilitated trough the explicit traceability support provided by our solution. Major changes in process models can affect the definition of business services. Reference models would assist the identification of new business services. Changes in elements from the AAL layer directly affect the definition of technical services. These changes might involve adaptations of existing business services. Despite the different nature in the mentioned changes, the explicit trace links between elements from different layers make those alterations traceable. This characteristic of the approach contributes positively to the modifiability of the final service-centric software solution.

The architectural approach presented in this paper has emerged from previous industrial work, together with the analysis of a wide rage of systems and methods for development of large scale systems. The authors have been involved in service based solutions projects for mining, governmental and e-learning domains, where coherence between business and software, and maintainability of architectures were key aspects.

5 Related Work

Methodologies such as those presented in [16] and [5] provide similar guidelines to design service centric architectures. We go beyond, incorporating modelling and traceability support to preserve coherence between business and software aspects. We also consider architectural abstractions in the form of reference models and patterns to enhance the final software solution. In [13], the authors use patterns and patterns primitives for process-oriented integration of services, however the considered patterns are at service composition level. The use of this kind of patterns are suitable during the last activities of our proposed development process. In [16] service identification is driven by the analysis of use cases and organisational units decomposition. We use business reference models to decompose the business domain of interest, abstracting the identification of services from a particular snapshot describing a temporal situation of the business. Note that the selected reference models in our approach are application independent. Software companies might also provide business service definitions based on reference models, however they often relate these definitions to their own software applications offer. The authors in [14] introduce a framework that incorporates reusable architectural decision models as design methodology for service realisation. Architectural decision models in our approach can help particular decision such as for example the election of a particular reference model or patterns, thus complementing our proposed framework.

6 Conclusion

Methodologies for EAI based on SOA are still maturing. In practice, most approaches start from the application level to afterwards adjust their designs to business levels. In this paper we have presented an architectural approach driven by business models while taking into account the constraints imposed by existing legacy application from the beginning of the architecture development process.

Coherence between business models and its supporting software was provided by a modelling framework and supporting techniques. The considered modelling notation provide graphical support and consistency, inherited from the selected modelling languages. Business reference models and patterns are used as guidelines to identify software services and to early recognise dependencies between services. Some of the activities of the layered architecture development process has the potential of been automated. Automation during transformation activities can increase the quality of software products, since human errors could be avoided. (Semi-)automatic pattern identification could reduce the time used during analysis activities and could help to inexperienced architects and business analysts to understand the business domain and previously proven architecture design solutions. Our future work includes efforts to automate some steps during the transformation and identification activities of the proposed architecture framework. Graph based formalization shall give the basis for consistency.

References

1. Lee, R.G. and Dale, B.G.: Business Process Management: A Review and Evaluation. BPM Journal 4(3) pp.214-225. Emerald (1998)
2. Aalst, W.M.P., Hofstede, A.H.M., Weske, M., Business Process Management: A Survey. In: Aalst, W.M.P., et al., (eds.). LNCS, Vol. 2678, pp. 1-12. Springer (2003)
3. Hohpe, G., Woolf, B.: Enterprise Integration Patterns. Addison-Wesley (2004)
4. Erl, T.: Service-oriented Architecture: Concepts, Technology, and Design. Prentice Hall (2004)
5. Papazoglou, M.P., Heuvel, W.J.: Service-Oriented Design and Development Methodology. Int. J. of Web Engineering and Technology (IJWET) 2(4) pp.412-442. Inderscience (2006)
6. Gamma, E., Helm, R., Johnson, R., Vlissides, J.: Design Patterns: Elements of Reusable Object-Oriented Software. Addison-Wesley (1995)
7. Business Process Modeling Notation Specification, version 1.1, OMG. Available at: http://www.omg.org/spec/BPMN/1.1/
8. Unified Modeling Language (Infrastructure and Superstructure), version 2.1.1, OMG. Available at: http://www.omg.org/spec/UML/2.1.2/
9. Bass, L., Clements, P., Kazman, R.: Software Architecture in Practice. Addison-Wesley (2004)
10. Eriksson, H. E. and Penker, M.: Business Modeling with UML: Business Patterns at Work. John Wiley & Sons. (1998)
11. Garlan, D., Schmerl, B., Architecture-driven Modelling and Analysis. In: Cant, T. (ed.) ACM Int. Conf. Proc. Series, Vol. 248, pp. 3-17. ACM (2006)
12. NACHA, The Electronic Payments Association. Available at: http://www.nacha.org
13. Zdun, U., Hentrich, C., Dustdar, S.: Modeling Process-driven and Service-oriented Architectures using Patterns and Pattern Primitives. ACM Trans. Web 1(3) pp.14:1-14:44 (2007)
14. Zimmermann, O., Koehler, J., Leymann, F.: Architectural Decision Models as Micro-Methodology for Service-Oriented Analysis and Design. In: Lubke, D. (ed.) CEUR-WS Proc. Vol. 244, pp.46-60 (2007)
15. Bengtsson, P., Lassing, N., Bosch, J., and van Vliet, H.: Architecture-level Modifiability Analysis (ALMA). J. of Systems and Software 69(1-2) pp.129-147 (2004)
16. Arsanjani, A.: Service-oriented Modeling and Architecture. Available at: http://www-128.ibm.com/developerworks/webservices/library/ws-soa-design1/

A LONGITUDINAL PERSPECTIVE ON CRITICAL ISSUES IN THE MANAGEMENT OF INFORMATION SYSTEMS IN LARGE ORGANISATIONS

Eamonn Caffrey, Joe McDonagh

School of Business, Trinity College Dublin,
Ireland
{ecaffrey, jmcdongh @tcd.ie}

Abstract. This paper assesses the literature on critical information systems (IS) management issues from a longitudinal perspective. Since the early 1980s, critical issues research has been a focus for many researchers with a view to contributing to both academia and practice. Critical issues in IS management were first studied in the United States, identifying the important concerns of IS management with subsequent studies turning their attention to Europe and Asia. Studies take a comparative perspective on critical issues across geographic and economic boundaries noting significant differences between developed and developing regions in particular. Studies over the last three decades has contributed to a cumulative body of knowledge which suggests that IS management is bedevilled with a consistent pattern of recurring issues across geographic boundaries which have persisted through time. Results of the study are helpful in pointing management towards a standardised set of critical issues for continuous focus.

Keywords: Information Systems; Information Systems Management; Key Issues; Top Management Concerns

Introduction

The continuous evolution of information systems (IS) management since the early 1980's has brought about a number of key issues for IS managers, executive management teams, end-users and organisation's on the whole. Today, IS, an important component in the management and survival of organisations dependent on it for support and competitive advantage (Porter and Millar, 1985; Cash et al., 1992). The rapidly changing business environment accompanied by the emergence of diverse technologies (Cash et al., 1992; Watson et al., 1997; Khandelwal, 2001; Luftman, 2005) result in many challenges facing both IS functions and management of organisations. A number of academic studies focusing on the key issues of IS management have emerged since 1980.

This paper reviews twenty six IS management key issue studies carried out between 1980 and 2006. Its purpose is to examine the concept and nature of key issues in IS management, assess the different dimensions that can impact IS issue results and to identify the IS issues that persistently appear as top management concerns, issues that feature consistently over a period of almost three decades of IS issue research.

Studies selected in this review begin with the earliest IS key issue survey performed by Harris and Ball (1980), results published in 1982, to Ilfinedo's (2006) study on IS management key issues for Estonia. This analysis of IS key issues takes a broad perspective by consolidating the results from each study and ranks the top ten issues that appear most frequently and considered by top management as their most important IS concerns. The findings indicate that irrespective of the organisation, industry, sector, or region, issues first noted when IS management studies begun in 1980 still feature today as the critical issues dominating management concerns and resources.

What is a Key Issue in IS Management

A key issue is an opportunity, threat, or problem associated with the effective use of information systems (IS) in the organisation (Yang, 1996). Key issues are concerned with the important viewpoints of IS management, the challenges or problems that IS management face and consider most difficult to solve.
An organisation's IS management practices are contingent upon both the role that IS serves within the organisation and the manner by which IS resources are made available to users. Together, these contextual factors comprise an organisation's internal IS environment. As this environment changes, IS management practices and research efforts must also change (Boynton and Zmud, 1987) prompting a never-ending stream of IS management key issues.

Purpose of Key Issue Studies

Over the past three decades a number of studies have been concerned with identifying the key issues facing IS management and executives in large-scale organisations. To understand what is important in IS at any given time according to Badri (1992) is dependent on both the technology and environment at the time. Therefore, regular assessment of the key issues confronting IS management is a necessary task. The results of IS critical issue studies therefore serve to support and guide IS management in their planning activities, to prepare in advance instead of acting when things happen (Brancheau et al., 1996; Clark, 1992; Watson et al, 1997). Organisations deciding what long-term investments to make for competitive advantage and future success must be based on informed choices. Described by Niederman et al. (1991), the primary purpose of IS key issue studies is to determine the IS management issues expected to be most important over the medium term (3-5 years) therefore most deserving of time and resource investment.

The results represent the future trends and aimed at providing useful direction for the IS community in order to serve their organisation economically, efficiently, and effectively. More simply, key issue studies are a guide to IS management and executives on where to focus their talent, what technologies and applications are en vogues and what areas of the business to invest IS capital expenditure.

Extant Studies in IS Management

We examine twenty six IS key issue research studies from 1980 to 2006 (see table 1). The studies enlist the views of knowledgeable practitioners from both the IT and non-IT (business managers) fields across a range of industries and sectors (public and private). The studies were carried out using a range of different research methodologies. Research was performed spanning different countries, and regions, some studies took a purely international perspective investigating IS management issues across a number of countries.

Past studies identify the emergence of new key issues, classify and rank the most important issues and outline the business drivers responsible for bringing about major shifts in the management of IS.

Table 1 presents the key issue studies selected for this review and captures the type of research method used, the industry sector, and the profile of research participants.

Table 1: IS Management Key Issue Studies (1982-2006)

Year	Publication	Article	Author	Method	Research	
					Sector	Profile
2006	Journal of Global Information Technology Management	Key Information Systems Management Issues in Estonia for the 2000s and A Comparative Analysis	Ifinedo, P.	Delphi (2 rounds)	Estonian Information Technology Society Members	Academics & IS Professionals
2005	Benchmarking: An International Journal	A Benchmarking framework for information systems management issues in Kuwait	Alshaway, A.H., Ali, J.M.H. & Hasan, M.H.	Three-phase protocol (Interview)	Public & Private	Senior IS Executives
2003	Journal of Global Information Technology Management	Key Issues in Information Systems Management: A Comparative Study of Academics and Practitioners in Thailand	Pimchangthong, D., Plaisent, M. & Bernard, P.	Q-methodology	Public, Private and State Enterprise Organisations	Academics & IS Professionals
2001	Information Resources Management Journal	Key Issues in IS Management in Norway: An Empirical Study Based on Q Methodology	Gottschalk, P.	Q-methodology	Public and Private Organisations	IT Managers
2000	Proceedings of the Information Resource Management Association International Conference, Alaska, 2000	Behind the Celtic Tiger: Key Issues in the Management of Information Technology in Ireland in the Late 1990's	McDonagh, J. & Harbison, A.	Two-phase protocol (Questionnaire)	Large-scale Public & Private Companies	Senior IT Managers
1999	Information Resources Management	Critical IS Issues in the Network Era	Kim, Y. & Kim Y.	Questionnaire	Fortune 500 and Academic Institutions	IT Executives

39

Year	Journal	Title	Authors	Method	Sample	Respondents
1999	International Journal of Information Management	MIS key issues in Taiwan's enterprises	Chou, H.W. & Jou, S.B.	Two-part questionnaire	Members of Information Management Association	IT Managers
1997	Journal of Management Information Systems	Key Issues in Information Systems Management: An International Perspective	Watson, R.T., Kelly, G.G., Galliers, R.D. & Brancheau, J.C.	Secondary data analysis	Public and Private Organisations	IT Managers
1997	Journal of Strategic Information Systems	Information systems management issues in Central America: a multinational and comparative study	Mata, F.J. & Fuerst, W.L.	Single-round field survey (Semi-structured interview)	Multinational Organisations	Senior IT Executives
1996	Information & Management	Key issues in information systems management: a Delphi study in Slovenia	Dekleva, A. & Zupancic, J.	Delphi technique (4 rounds)	330 Slovenian Companies	IT Managers
1996	MIS Quarterly	Key Issues in Information Systems Management: 1994-95 SIM Delphi Results	Brancheau, J.C., Janz, B.D. & Wetherbe, J.C.	Delphi method (3 rounds)	SIM Institutional members	Senior IT & Executive Management
1996	Information & Management	Key issues in the management of information systems: A Hong Kong perspective	Moores, .T.T	Survey	300 Assorted organisations	IT Managers
1994	Journal of Information Technology	Coping with information technology? How British executives perceive the key information systems management issues in the mid-1990s	Galliers, R.D., Merali, Y. & Spearing, L.	Survey	Times 1000 Companies	Senior IT & Executive Management
1993	Journal of Global Information Management	Critical Issues of IS Management in Hong Kong: A Cultural Comparison	Burn, J., Saxena, K.B.C., Ma, L. & Cheung, H.K.	Organisational Cultural Audit	Government, public & private	98 Middle/Senior Managers

Year	Journal	Title	Authors	Method	Organisations	Respondents
1993	Journal of Strategic Information Systems	Key Information Technology Issues in Estonia	Dexter, A.S., Janson, M.A., Kiudorf, E. & Laast-Laas, J.	Question naire	Public & Private Organisations	IT Managers
1992	International Journal of Information Management	Critical Issues in Information Systems Management: An International Perspective	Badri, M.A.	Self-administered questionnaire	Private Organisations	CIOs
1991	MIS Quarterly	Information Systems Management Issues for the 1990s	Niederman, F., Brancheau, J.C. & Wetherbe, J.C.	Delphi method	241 SIM Institutional and Board memers	IS Executives
1991	Journal of Management Information Systems	Identification of Key International Information Systems Issues in J.S.-Based Multinational Corporations	Deans, P.C., Karwan, K.R., Goslar, M.D., Ricks, D.A. & Toyne, B.	Two-phase methodology	588 multinational corporations	Executive-level MIS managers
1991	Information & Management	Key issues in information systems management	Watson, R.T. & Brancheau, J.C.	Previous study review	Public & Private Organisations	IT &Executive Management
1991	MIS Quarterly	Key Information Systems Management Issues for the Public Sector	Caudle, S.L., Gorr, W.L. & Newcomer, K.E.	Question naire	Public sector organisations	Executive & IS Branch officials
1989	The Australian Computer Journal	Key Issues in information systems management: An Australian perspective-1988	Watson, R.T.	Delphi study (3 rounds)	Top 200 public & private organisations	IS Executives
1988	Journal of Information Technology	Managing Information Systems in 1987: the Top Issues for IS Managers in the UK	Parker, T. & Idundun, M.	Survey	100 largest UK Companies	IS Executives
1987	MIS Quarterly	Key Issues in Information Systems Management	Crancheau, J.C. & Wetherbe, J.C.	Delphi method (3 rounds)	SIM Institutional & Board members	IS Executives & General Managers

1986	MIS Quarterly	1985 Opinion Survey of MIS Managers: Key Issues	Hartog, C. & Herbert, M.	Delphi method (4 rounds)	SIM & MISRC members	MIS Management Businesses & Government
1984	MIS Quarterly	Key Information Systems Issues for the 1980's	Dickson, G.W., Leitheiser, R.L., Wetherbe, J.C. & Nechis, M.	Delphi method (4 rounds)	SIM Institutional & Board members	IS Executives & General Managers
1982	MIS Quarterly	SMIS Members: A Membership Analysis	Ball, L. & Harris, R.	Question naire	SIM Institutional & Board members	IS Executives & General Managers

Key Issue Research Methods

Two popular research approaches amongst researchers of IS management issues is the Delphi technique and Q-sort method, adopted for ten of the key issue studies. Questionnaires, surveys, and interviews are also widely used across the studies chosen.

Figure 1: Key Issue Research Methods

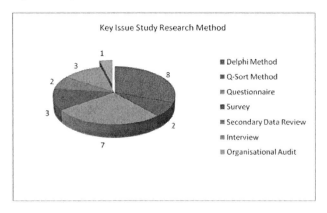

Geographical Regions of Key Issue Studies

In figure 2, we see the breakdown by country or region for the twenty six studies. IS management key issue studies first started in 1980 in the USA, this theme continued with the USA leading the way until an investigation was carried out on IS issues in the UK in 1988. The USA leads as the main contributor towards key issue research however, figure 2 clearly shows a transparent cross-section of studies have now been conducted around the world, allowing us to gain a true international flavour of IS management key issues.

Figure 2: Geographical Regions of Key Issue Studies

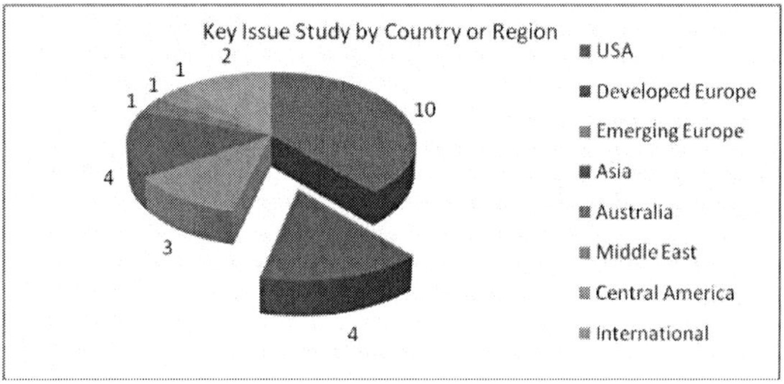

Participant Profiles in IS Management Key Issue Research

All studies focused on investigating IS management issues in large-scale organisations. 50% of the studies carried out research selecting a mix of private and public large scale organisations simultaneously. Only one study focused solely on examining key issues in the public sector. In the USA, members of the Society for Information Management (SIM) participated in key issue research on six different occasions. SIM member selectection was made on the basis of size and scale of member organisation and exposure to IS management trends, namely IS executive management, senior corporate management and board members.

Figure 3: Participant Profile in Key Issue Studies

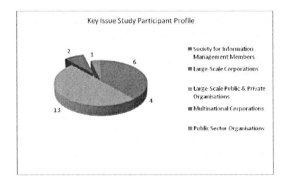

Dimensions of Extant Studies in IS Management

Over time, the studies cover a range of key issue research domains. These domains vary by region, country, economic environment, organisation and industry type. The effects of economic development and national culture along with the stage of IS development by region can cause differences to the types and status of IS issues faced by management. In terms of measuring the importance of IS management issues, the studies show the following dimensions can influence the direction of IS management in large organisations thus impacting on the level of importance of IS management issues. We observe differences based on time, geographical position, political, legal, economical, and technological status.

Business Drivers

Business requirements for speed, flexibility, and responsiveness, are driving the importance of IS issues. The move from industrial enterprise to an information enterprise, the globalisation of business, changing global labour markets and increasing volatility of business environments all impact significantly on the role of IS management. Such business changes suggest a sustained growth in new applications and a continuing high interest by senior managers in where and how the IS budget is spent (Benjamin and Blunt, 1992).

Developed versus Developing Countries

Researchers suggest key issue relevance should change from infrastructure issues to operational issues to strategic issues as a nation progresses through different stages of economic and IT development (Palvia et al., 1992). Previous studies indicate that politics, law, culture, economics, technology infrastructure, and the availability of skilled personnel can greatly influence the nature of IS management issues between developed and developing countries.

National Culture

Cultural differences between regions can result with differences in IS effects. These differences in culture can be explained by applying the five dimensions of national culture: power distance, uncertainty avoidance, individualism, masculinity, and time orientation (Hofstede, 1991). Deklava and Zupancic (1996) identified profound differences in the IS management issues between Slovenia and the USA.

Political and Legal Environment

Issues considered critical and even those less so can be greatly influenced by the political and legal status of a country or region. Some examples of how national governments have had an impact on IS issues demonstrate this prominent dimension for consideration. When the US considered making parts of the internet privately-owned, this caused concern amongst many. In India, the government's pro-active application of technology to attract inward investment influenced the status of IS within the country. The entry to the EU for many eastern European countries impacted on business and the application of communications and technology (Watson et al., 1997).

Industry Sector

In an attempt to gain greater clarity and a degree of consensus on the nature of IS key issues, a study found that there exists considerable differences across manufacturing, services, and non-profit industry sectors (Niederman et al., 1991). Some of the differences noted that key issue views held by Universities (non-profit) were not characterised by competitive advantage, IS control, systems development and application portfolio, important key issue views for manufacturing and service industry organisations. IS management for the service industry held a much higher view on applications development when compared with counterparts in the manufacturing field. One possible reason for this difference suggested that industries can be classified into different strategic quadrants and that firms in those industries take different levels of strategic orientation toward both their existing and planned application portfolios (McFarlan et al., 1983).

Private versus Public Sector

Three key differences exist between public and private organisations: environmental factors; organisation/environment transactions; and internal structure and processes (Rainey et al., 1976).

In terms of the IS management issues, public sector organisations do not pursue the goal of using IS to gain competitive advantage, an alternative counterpart was proposed for the public sector, that of technology transfer, to find new ways to increase the transfer and sharing and exchange of data across similar agency functions. In a study of public sector IS management issues, it's interesting to note that while there are distinct differences between public and private organisations, the study discovered that comprehensive planning, long-term planning, data security, integration of technologies, and information requirements identification are some of the most important IS issues within the public sector (Caudle, 1991).

As with the top ranked IS issues in this paper, similar issues are considered important to the public sector. In a separate study reviewing IS issues across public and private sector organisations in Estonia, the research found that organisations from both sectors hold comparable views on the key issues in IS management (Ifinedo, 2006).

Global IT

The rapid globalisation of business and the increased role of IS in shaping corporate strategy, indicates that global IS has become a topic of considerable importance to information systems practitioners (Ives and Jarvenpaa, 1991). In their study, the authors identified four groups of key issues classified as linking IS and business strategy, information technology platforms, international data sharing, and the cultural environment. More pronounced work was later done in which a model was introduced for global IS issues analysis. The model includes seven categories of global IS management issues: IS business relationships; human resources and IS management; IS quality and reliability issues; internal effectiveness measurement; end-user computing; technology infrastructure; and systems development (Aguila et al., 2002). It was discovered that the challenges faced by senior IS executives in different parts of the world introduces a wide range of IS management issues nevertheless, the context of these issue groups are much the same to the groups mentioned earlier, especially the contribution made by Niederman.

The study went further to suggest that key issues in global IS management can be influenced by two types of contextual/global factors. The first is country-specific variables; level of economic development of the country, political and regulatory factors, and cultural, variables mentioned above in the context of developed and developing countries. The second variable set is firm-specific and includes the type of firm and industry, global strategies, and global business and IS strategy.

In China for example, some critical issues for consideration include technology transfer, global environment changes, organisational structure, business finance, and education and training. Business collaboration leads to increased global alliances, joint research and development and production projects but the complexities of technology and knowledge transfer across international boundaries have led to misunderstandings in the operation and implementation of international joint venture projects (Li-Hua and Khalil, 2006).

IS Management Issue Classification and Groups: Underlying Constructs

Three separate studies led to the classification of key issues. The classification options are *Management* and *Technology* (Brancheau and Wetherbe, 1987); *Planning* and *Control* (Watson, 1989); and *Internal* and *External* (Hirschheim, 1988). Each IS issue can be classified in accordance with its relevant position to the IS environment, function and impact on the organisation and business strategy. According to Palvia and Basu (1999), identifying the underlying constructs related to IS management issues is more meaningful that reporting on each particular issue, considered more beneficial because the nature of IS activities requires management to take a holistic view of the organisation. It's important to not only be concerned with the specific IS issues that are prevalent but to consider these in conjunction with the technology, business strategies, organisation structure, management processes, and employees and their roles (Earl, 1992; Somogyi and Galliers, 1987; Alshawaf et al., 2005)
Management (M) issues deal with policy, strategy, structure, accountability and human resource. *Technology* (T) issues tend to deal with the specification, acquisition, development, use and protection of information technologies (Brancheau and Wetherbe, 1987). *Planning* (P) issues tend to take a long-range strategic view of a problem whereas *Control* (C) issues take a mid-range tactical view (Watson, 1989) . *Internal* (I) matters are concerned with the management of the IS organisation and related technologies, while

External (E) matters are concerned with management of the business as a whole (Hirschheim et al., 1988).

Based on this classification scheme, key issues from a study in 1990 were organised into four groups: Business Relationship (BR); Technology Infrastructure (TI); Internal Effectiveness (IE); and Technology Application (TA), reflecting major thrusts in IS management (Niederman et al., 1991).

Further to Niederman's work, Caudle, (1991); Ives, (1991); Hartog, (1996); Yang, (1996); Palvia and Basu, (1996); and Alshawaf et al., (2005) propose entirely different groups. However, Niederman's table of IS issue groups is preferred, not only for its simplicity and underlying constructs but also for its grasp to encapsulate all of the dominant key themes found in the majority of key issue studies. Moreover, it provides the transparency to categorise IS issues into distinct groups and classify their position to the IS environment and impact on the organisation and business strategy (M/T); (P/C); and (I/E).

Towards a Synthesis of Key Issue Studies

An analysis of the studies shown earlier in table 1 allows us to identify and illustrate the top ten IS management key issues. The basis for issue selection was made by reviewing all top ten key issues in each of twenty six studies, then mapping the frequency and rank for each issue. The analysis found twenty recurring issues from twenty six studies (see appendix A). In terms of issue frequency, the top ten issues identified appear as a top ten issue in more than 50% of the twenty six studies. Issues are measured by the rate of occurrence for each. In table 2, we can see that the rate of occurrence extends from 54% (Information Architecture, 14 studies) issue #10, to 88% (Strategic Planning, 23 studies) issue #1.

While the primary measurement tool for ranking issues is based on the rate of occurrence, table 1 also illustrates the median, mode, and average rank. Figure 4 (see appendix B) represents the level of importance across the different types of measurement rank.

Table 2: Perceived Most Important Key Issues in Information Systems Management

Rank	1	2	3	4	5	6	7	8	9	10	Region	Study Reference
Issue	Strategic Planning	Data Resource	IS Organisational Alignment	Software Development	IS Human Resource	Competitive Advantage	Responsive IT Infrastructure	IS Effectiveness & Measurement	Organisational Learning	Information Architecture		
Issue Rank in Past Studies	1	2	-	4	-	-	3	6	-	-	Estonia	Ifinedo, 2006
	6	3	-	-	8	-	4	-	-	-	Kuwait	Alshawat et al., 2005
	2	7	-	4	3	-	1	-	7	10	Thailand	Pimchangthon et al., 2009
	2	6	7	-	5	10	9	1	8	-	Ireland	McDonagh et al., 2001
	3	10	1	7	6	2	5	8	-	4	Norway	Gottschalk, 2001
	-	6	5	10	7	4	8	-	-	-	Taiwan	Chou et al., 1999
	8	-	10	6	-	1	5	-	-	7	USA	Kim et al., 1999
	3	2	5	10	8	4	-	-	9	1	International	Watson et al., 1997
	2	6	-	3*	5	1	-	-	9	-	Central America	Mata et al., 1997
	3	-	4	-	2	-	8	10	5	7	Slovenia	Dekleva et al., 1996
	1	7	9	-	8	2	1	6	-	4	USA	Brancheau et al., 1996
	3	2	10	1	7	5	-	6	8	4	Hong Kong	Moores, 1996
	1	2	3	4*	-	7	-	9	10	4*	UK	Galliers et al., 1994
	2	5	3	10	1	6*	-	4	-	-	Hong Kong	Burn et al., 1993
	-	10	-	-	-	-	6	2	-	8	Estonia	Dexter, 1993
	1	-	5	9*	-	4	8	7	3	-	GCC	Badri, 1992
	3	2	7	9	4	8	6	-	5	1	USA	Niederman et al., 1991
	-	8	-	-	-	7	3	-	-	-	USA	Deans et al., 1991
	1	8*	2	10	6*	3	1	-	6*	5	International	Watson et al., 1991
	2	6	5	10	-	3	-	-	-	3	USA	Caudle et al., 1991
	1	9	5	4	2	7	1	-	10	3	Australia	Watson, 1989
	3	9	1	10	6	-	-	5	-	8	UK	Parker et al., 1987
	1	7	5	-	-	2	-	9	3	8	USA	Brancheau et al., 1987
	1	4	2	3	-	-	7	9	-	-	USA	Hartog et al., 1986
	1	9	7	4	8	-	-	5	6	-	USA	Dickson et al., 1984

50

	1	-	9	-	7	-	-	2	6	-
Rat e of	8%	85%	80%	69%	6 5%	62%	58%	58%	54%	54%
Me dian Rank	2	6	5	7	6	4	5	6	7	4
Mo de Rank	1	2	5	1)	8	2	1	6	8	4
Ave rage Rank	3. 04	5.8	5.25	6.8	5. 43	4.57	5	5.93	6.84	5

*Denotes jointly ranked issue

From the results shown in table 2, we can gauge the frequency of each issue. The table highlights the issues that are a regular feature to key issue research, spanning no less than twenty five years. Strategic planning, data resource, IS organisational alignment, software development and IS human resource are issues frequently noted.

Key issue focus can shift and fluctuate periodically from a management focus to a technical one. It was noted by Hartog and Herbert (1986) that the results of their research findings in 1985 suggest that IS management is more orientated to corporate than to technical issues. As the field of IS entered the 1990s, a new trend observed the rising importance of technology infrastructure issues occupying three of the top ten slots including the highest position (Niederman et al., 1991). By 1999, technical priorities continuously evolved and changed while managerial issues remained constant (Kim and Kim, 1999). The constant emergence of new technologies, shorter life cycle of technologies and fast growing advances in communication networks gave rise to a continuous stream of new technical priorities.

Top Management Concerns

The findings made here reflect similarly to a study that examined the long-term trends of key issues from a series of six surveys of IS professionals during 1980 to 1995 (Kim and Kim, 1999). In all six surveys, four issues consistently appeared in the top ten IS issues for managers: IS strategic planning; data resource management; IS alignment within the organisation; and information architecture. The results found here support the findings of Kim and Kim (1999). The four key issues they noted as top management concerns between 1980 to 1995 are found in this study, ranked # 1, 2, 3, and 10 respectively, adding further validity to the fact that the top issues in IS management don't evaporate over time.

Strategic Planning

Strategic planning is ranked the #1 issue for IS management, appearing as a top ten key issue in twenty three of twenty six (88%) journal studies, in many cases ranked among the top three issues (Brancheau and Wetherbe, 1987; Niederman et al., 1991; Palvia et al., 1996; Kim and Kim, 1999; Gottschalk, 2001). This underlines its ongoing importance for IS management. IS strategic planning requires close alignment with business plans (Certo and Peter, 1988). Effective planning depends heavily on appropriate IS organisation alignment (#3) and provides direction for software development (#4), technology infrastructure (#7), and information architecture (#10) (Niederman et al., 1991). Its persistence as the most regularly featured top ten IS issue clearly indicates the necessity for further inquiry.

Effective Use of Data Resources

The transition from a world of industrial economies to information-based economies and businesses shifting from local to global markets give rise to the fact why this issue has grown in importance over the years. Many organisations store increasing volumes of information from customers, suppliers, financial partners, and the economic environment (Frenzel, 1991). Intelligently combining these disparate streams of information for purposes of making better decisions, gaining insight into potentially useful innovations, and streamlining operations without being overwhelmed by information overload remains both a major challenge and opportunity (Niederman et al., 1991). Additionally, the increased globalisation of businesses places a tremendous demand for information that is needed for executive decision-making creating a "must-have" for major corporations (Kumar and Palvia, 2001).

IS Organisational Alignment

Today's high-speed business changes (Allen and Boynton, 1991) require the IS organisation to align with the business strategy to be more effective in supporting organisational change. Organisations change themselves to compete in the new business environment through business process reengineering, information empowerment, and organisational restructuring (Kim and Kim, 1999). It means "*applying IS in an appropriate and timely way, in harmony and collaboration with business needs, goals, and strategies*" (Luftman et al., MIS Quarterly Executive, 2006, 5(2), p. 83).

Software Development

Organisations can choose to develop applications in-house or turn to packaged application solutions or external systems development resources to meet their needs. During the 1980/90s, a number of computer-aided software engineering (CASE) tools were designed and intended to improve the effectiveness of application development. CASE tools proved to be most effective in the initial stages of application development, that is, in requirements definition and application specification as contrasted to coding and testing (Fried, 1993). Additionally, such tools do not specifically support the maintenance of older or legacy applications that remain critical in supporting the organisation's processes and information flow. When developing new applications, forecasting the lifetime cost of the application can be more accurately projected using high-level CASE tools and methodology. Fried states that the maintenance and enhancement cost for running applications can be as much as 70% of the total lifetime cost of the application. Knowing the true cost; application development, testing, and implementation, along with the ongoing enhancement and quality maintenance cost is an important issue when determining what applications to develop and support and the decision whether to develop in-house or to look externally.

IS Human Resource

IS human resource, ranked #5 and among the top issues since 1982. The need to stay on top of rapid changes in both business and technology conspire to keep human resources a top issue (Brancheau et al., 1996) Staying current with emerging technologies and a continuing emphasis on developing business skills such as teamwork and leadership contributes largely to an organisations ability to make effective use of IS. To stay on top, organisations need to attract, develop and retain IS professionals (Luftman, 2006). As an organisation's IS headcount rises this can point to a number of reasons for its growing importance: buoyant economy; organisation takes the long-term view that it's essential to invest in professional IS staff; globalisation of the IS function; and the dynamic business environment and constant changes in technology place growing demands on IS resources.

Competitive Advantage

In 1983, competitive advantage was not salient enough to stand alone as a distinct issue, by 1986 however using IS for competitive advantage was ranked second in importance, having exploded on the IS scene in recent years (Brancheau and Wetherbe, 1987). Through creativity and innovation, new opportunities are recognised, the development and implementation of IS to benefit from these opportunities is what creates a level of differentiation and provides an advantage. New capabilities are developed over periods of time when technology has been tightly integrated into the organisation's core business activities and strategic planning.

Developing Responsive Technology Infrastructure

Building a responsive IT infrastructure is considered a strategic issue, because such an infrastructure not only supports existing business applications but also facilitates timely response to changing business conditions (Palvia and Basu, 1999). The linkage of IT and business requirements tie these two together. It is important for organisations to follow an architecture-based approach (Tan et al., 1997) which brings together the IS function and business organisation to move in the same direction.

IS Effectiveness and Measurement

IS investment can give firms a basis for increased coordination and control or can provide direct competitive advantage (Ives and Jarvenpaa, 1991). How far an organisation progresses, and the benefits it obtains from doing so, will depend more upon its ability to identify strategic goals and to manage than upon any technical or economic factor. The major reason that the benefits of IS implementation have been slow in coming is that organisational change in not adequately managed. Even with a commitment to change management, companies are likely to find that people's inability to change, not technology, is the limiting factor (Benjamin and Blunt, 1992).

Organisational Learning

Top management continue to believe that successful organisations will be those that continue to make most effective use of new and emerging IS. However, the introduction of each new technology, the continuous learning demands on how best to use the information resources and integrate into the organisation signals the start of a new learning curve (Bouldin, 1989).

Developing Information Architecture

Information value arises as the difference between a decision maker's payoff in the absence of information relative to what can be obtained in its presence (Banker and Kaufmann, 2004). Information architecture emerged as the #1 issue in 1986. The information architecture is a high-level map for guiding and directing the information requirements of an organisation. In its pure form, the mapping of information is independent of personnel staffing, organisation structures and technology platforms (Brancheau et al., 1989). A well designed architecture can provide the basis for developing a responsive, coordinated and long-lasting set of business applications. The importance of developing an information architecture that supports the overall IS of an organisation is critical, it supports all of the top key issues listed. It is defined as the "*major information categories used within an enterprise and their relationships to business processes. It is also needed to guide applications development and facilitate the integration and sharing of data*" (Pimchangthong et al., Journal of Global Information Management, 2003, 6(4), p.37).

Classification of Key Issues

Taking Niederman's grouping labels and classifying the issues listed in table 2, we find that strategic planning (#1), data resource management (#2), IS organisational alignment (#3), competitive advantage (#6), and organisational learning (#9) are grouped collectively as business relationship issues. This suggests the group of business relationship issues should be the major thread for IS management focus given the superior ranking of these issues.

Table 3: Key Issue Classification

Issue Classification					
Rank	Issue Name	M/T	P/C	I/E	Group
1	Strategic Planning	M	P	E	BR
2	Data Resource Management	M	C	E	BR
3	IS Organisational Alignment	M	C	E	BR
4	Software Development	T	C	I	IE
5	IS Human Resource	M	C	I	IE
6	Competitive Advantage	M	P	E	BR
7	Responsive IT Infrastructure	T	C	I	TI
8	IS Effectiveness & Measurement	M	C	I	IE
9	Organisational Learning	M	C	E	BR
10	Information Architecture	T	P	I	TI

Source: Adopted from Niederman et al., (1991)

While this classification and grouping framework for issues has served the IS community for over fifteen years, it clearly demonstrates its relevance holds true even today as the cluster of business relationship issues dominate the top ten issues found here.

Conclusion

This paper reviewed the results of twenty six IS management key issue studies performed across many different geographical boundaries. From the results of these studies we have been able to compile a set of top ten key issues that are prevalent over time and affect all regional territories. The IS management issue, strategic planning, is the top management concern for IS executives. The group of business relationship issues covers 50% of the top ten issues.

Key issue research makes an important contribution to the field of IS in helping to confirm and guide the direction of management interests concerning IS and their organisation. Over the years, the results from a number of studies highlight that issues are both technical and managerial in nature. Issues can be of a broad or narrow time horizon. Management issues are long-term and continuous requiring a permanent focus. As technologies evolve so do technical issues however, a number of the same issues continuously draw attention from practitioners; strategic planning, data resource management, and IS alignment of the organisation. Issues that appear frequently among the top five views relate to how IS integrates, impacts, and responds to the fast changing nature of business and the direct relationship therein.

The type of issues facing an organisation or country can be influenced by a number of dimensions; the economic status of the country, the industry or sector of the organisation, national culture, legal, political and technological stage of development. Some similarity of views on key issues is shared between public and private sector organisations.

Growth in global business is driving global IT creating new challenges and issues for IS management. Overall, while key issues continue to be a major focus for management, a greater orientation towards globalisation is evident as more studies and research now take on an international perspective.

References

1. Allen, B.S. & Boynton, A.C. (1991) Information Architecture: In Search of Efficient Flexibility, MIS Quarterly, vol. 15, iss. 4, pp. 435-445
2. Badri, M.A. (1992) Critical Issues in Information Systems Management: An International Perspective, International Journal of Information Management, vol. 12, pp. 179-191
3. Ball, L. & Harris, R. (1982) SIM Members: A Membership Analysis, MIS Quarterly, vol. 6, iss.1, pp. 19-38
4. Banker, R.D. & Kaufmann, R.J. (2004) The Evolution of Research on Information Systems: A Fiftieth-Year Survey of the Literature in Management Science, Management Science, vol. 50, iss. 3, pp. 281-298
5. Benjamin, R. & Blunt, J. (1992) Critical IT Issues: The Next Ten Years, Sloan Management Review, vol. 33, iss. 4, pp. 7-19
6. Boynton, A.C. & Zmud, R.W. (1987) An Assessment of Critical Success Factors, Sloan Management Review, Vol. 25, No. 4, pp. 17-29
7. Brancheau, J.C., Janz, B.D. & Wetherbe, J.C. (1996) Key IS Issues in Information Systems Management: 1994-95 SIM Delphi Results, MIS Quarterly, vol. 20, iss. 2, pp. 225—242

8. Brancheau, J.C., Schuster, L. & March, S.T. (1989) Building and Implementing an Information Architecture, Data Base, vol.20, iss. 2, pp. 9 -17
9. Bruno-Britz, M. (2005) CEOs Have Love/Hate Relationship With IT", Bank Systems and Technology, vol. 42, iss. 10, p. 16
10. Burn, J., Saxena, K.B.C., Ma, L. & Cheung, H.K. (1993) Critical Issues of IS Management in Hong Kong: A Cultural Comparison, Journal of Global Information Management, vol. 1, no. 4, pp. 28-37
11. Cash, J.J., McFarlan, F.W., McKenney, J.L. & Applegate, L. (1992) Corporate Information Systems Management: Text and Cases, New York: Irwin Professional Publishers
12. Caudle, S. L., Gorr, W.L. & Newcomer, K.E. (1991) Key Information Management Issues for the Public Sector, MIS Quarterly, vol. 15, iss. 2, pp. 171-188
13. Certo, S.C. & Peter, J.P. (1988) Strategic Management, Random House, New York
14. Clark, T.D. Corporate Systems Management: an overview and research perspective, Communications of the ACM, vol. 35, iss. 2, pp. 60-75
15. Chou, H.W. & Jou, S.B. (1999) MIS key issues in Taiwan's enterprises, International Journal of Information Management, vol. 19, pp. 369-387
16. Deans, P.C., Karwan, K.R., Goslar, M.D., Ricks, D.A. & Toyne, B. (1991) Identification of Key International Information Systems Issues in U.S.-Based Multinational Corporations, Journal of Management Information Systems, vol. 7, no. 4, pp. 27-50
17. Deklava, S. & Zupancic, J. (1996) Key IS Issues in Information Systems Management: A Delphi Study in Slovenia, Information and Management, vol. 31, pp. 1-11
18. Del Aguila, A.R., Bruque, S. & Padilla, A. (2002) Global Information Technology Measurement and Organisational Analysis: Research Issues, Journal of Global Information Technology Management, vol. 5, no. 4, pp. 18-37
19. Dexter, A.S., Janson, M. A., Kiudorf, E. & Laast-Laas, J. (1993) Key Information Technology Issues in Estonia, Journal of Strategic Information Systems, vol. 2, no. 2, pp. 139-152
20. Dixon, P.J. & Darwin, J.A. (1989) Technology Issues Facing Corporate Management in the 1990s, MIS Quarterly, vol. 3, iss. 3, pp. 247-255
21. Earl, M.J. (1992) Putting information technology in its place: a polemic for the nineties, Journal of Information Technology, vol. 7, pp. 100-108
22. Frenzel, C.W. (1991) Information Technology Management, Boyd & Fraser, Boston, MA
23. Fried, L. (1993) Current IT trends and Business Issues: An Executive Briefing, Information Strategy. The Executive's Journal, vol. 2, pp. 16-25
24. Galliers, R.D., Merali, Y. & Spearing, L. (1994) Coping with information technology? How British executives perceive the key information systems management issues in the mid-1990s, Journal of Information Technology, vol. 9, pp. 223-238
25. Gottschalk, P. (2001) Key Issues in IS Management in Norway: An Empirical Study Based on Q Methodology, Information Resources Management Journal, vol. 14, no. 2, pp. 37-45
26. Hartog, C. & Herbert, M. (1986) 1985 Opinion Survey of MIS Managers: Key Issues, MIS Quarterly, vol. 10, iss. 4, pp. 351-361
27. Hirschheim, R., Earl, M., Feeney, D & Lockett, M. (1988) An exploration into the management of the information systems function: key issues and an evolutionary model, Information Technology Management for Productivity and Competitive Advantage, An IFIP TC-8 Open Conference, pp. 4.15-4.38
28. Hofstede, G. (1991) Cultures and Organizations: Software of the Mind, McGraw-Hill, New York

29. Ilfinedo, P. (2006) Key Information Systems Management Issues in Estonia for the 2000s and a Comparative Analysis, Journal of Global Information Technology Management, vol. 9, no. 2, pp. 22-44

30. Ives, B. & Jarvenpaa, S.L. (1991) Applications of Global Information Technology: Key Issues for Management, MIS Quarterly, vol. 15, iss. 1, pp. 33-49

31. Khandelwal, V.K. (2001) An Empirical Study of Misalignment between Australian CEOs and IT Managers, Journal of Strategic Information Systems, vol. 10, no. 1, pp. 15-28

32. Kim, Y. & Kim, Y. (1999) Critical IS Issues in the Network Era, Information Resources Management Journal, vol. 12, no. 4, pp. 14-23

33. Kumar, A. & Palvia, P. (2001) Key data management issues in a global executive information system, Industrial Management & Data Systems, vol. 101, no. 3/4, pp. 153-164

34. Li-Hua, R. & Khalil, T.M. (2006) Technology management in China: a global perspective and challenging issues, vol. 1, no. 1, pp. 9-26

35. Luftman, J. (2005) Key Issues for IT Executives 2004, MIS Quarterly Executive, vol. 4, iss. 2, pp. 269-285

36. Mata, F.J. & Fuerst, W.L. (1997) Information systems management issues in Central America: a multinational and comparative study, Journal of Strategic Information Systems, vol. 6, pp. 173-202

37. McDonagh, J. & Harbison, A. (2000) Behind the Celtic Tiger: Key Issues in the Management of Information Technology in Ireland in the Late 1990's, Proceedings of the Information Resource Management Association International Conference, Alaska (2000), pp. 197-201

38. Moores, T. (1996) Key issues in the management of information systems: A Hong Kong perspective, Information & Management, vol. 30, pp. 301-307

39. Moynihan, T. (1990) What Chief Executives and Senior Managers Want From Their IT Departments, MIS Quarterly, vol. 14, iss. 1, pp. 15-25

40. McFarlan, F.W., McKenney, J.L. & Pyburn, P. (1983) The Information Archipelago-Plotting a Course, Harvard Business Review, vol. 61, no. 1, pp. 145-156

41. Niederman, F., Brancheau, J.C. & Wetherbe, J.C. (1991) Information Systems Management Issues in the 1990's, MIS Quarterly, vol. 15, iss. 4, pp. 474-500

42. Palvia, P.C. & Basu, S.C. (1999) Information Systems Management Issues: Reporting and Relevance, Decision Sciences, vol. 30, iss. 1, pp. 273-290

43. Palvia, P., Rajagopalan, B., Kumar, A. & Kumar, N. (1996) Key Information Systems Issues: An Analysis of MIS Publications, Information Processing and Management, vol. 32, no.3, pp. 345-355

44. Palvia, P.C., Palvia, S.C. & Whitworth, J.E. (2002) Global information technology: a Meta analysis of key issues, Information and Management, vol. 39, pp. 403-414

45. Palvia, P.C., Palvia, S. & Zigili, R.M. (1992) Global information technology environment: key MIS issues in advanced and less-developed nations, The Global Issues of Information Technology Management, Idea Group Publishing, Harrisburg, PA. pp. 2-34

46. Parker, T & Idundun, M. (1988) Managing Information Systems in 1987: the Top Issues for IS Managers in the UK, Journal of Information Technology, vol. 3, no. 1, pp. 34-42

47. Porter, M.E. & Millar, V.E. (1985) How Information Gives You Competitive Advantage, Harvard Business Review, vol. 63, no. 1, pp. 149-160

48. Rainey, H., Backoff, R. & Levine, C. (1976) Comparing Public and Private Organisations, Public Administration Review, vol. 36, iss. 2, pp. 233-244

49. Six Top Information Systems Issues (1985) EDP Analyzer, Canning Publications Inc., vol. 23, no. 1, pp. 1-12

50. Somogyi, .EK. & Galliers, R.D. (1987) Information Technology in Business: From Data Processing to Strategic Information Systems, Journal of Information Technology, vol. 2, no.1, pp. 30-41
51. Tan, D.S. & Uijttenbrock, A.A. (1997) Information infrastructure management: A new role for IS managers, Information systems management, vol. 14, no. 4, pp. 33-41
52. UNCTAD, E-Commerce and Development Report (2003)
53. Watson R.T. (1989) Key issues in information systems management: an Australian perspective-1988, Australian Computer Journal, vol. 21, no. 3, pp. 118-129
54. Watson, R.T. & Brancheau, J.C. (1991) Key issues in information systems management: an international perspective, Information & Management, vol. 20, pp. 213-223
55. Watson, R.T., Kelly, G.G., Galliers, R.D. & Brancheau, J.C. (1997) Key IS Issues in Information Systems Management: An International Perspective, Journal of Management Information Systems, vol. 13, no. 4, pp. 91-115
56. Yang, H.L. (1996) Key Information Management Issues in Taiwan and the US, Information & Management, vol. 30, pp. 251-267

Appendix A

Table 4: Perceived Top 20 Recurring Issues in Information Systems Management

Rank	Key Issue	Rate of Occurrence	Median Rank	Mode Rank	Average Rank
1	Strategic Planning	88%	2	1	3.043
2	Data Resource	85%	6	2	5.809
3	IS Organisational Alignment	80%	5	5	5.25
4	Software Development	69%	7	10	6.8
5	IS Human Resource	65%	6	8	5.437
6	Competitive Advantage	62%	4	2	4.571
7	Responsive IT Infrastructure	58%	5	1	5
8	IS Effectiveness & Measurement	58%	6	6	5.933
9	Organisational Learning	54%	7	8	6.846
10	Information Architecture	54%	4	4	5
11	Network & Communications	50%	6	3	5.833
12	IS Security & Control	50%	5.5	6	4.916
13	End-User Computing	50%	5.5	8	5.1
14	Awareness Among Top Managers	35%	5	8	5
15	Role & Contribution of IS	23%	6	6	6.8
16	Disaster Recovery	15%	5.5	-	5.5
17	Distributed Systems	15%	6.75	-	7
18	Application Portfolio	15%	9	9	9
19	Executive Decision Support	15%	9.5	10	8.5
20	Electronic Data Interchange	4%	5	-	5

Appendix B

Figure 4: Perceived Most Important Key Issues in Information Systems Management - Rate of Occurrence

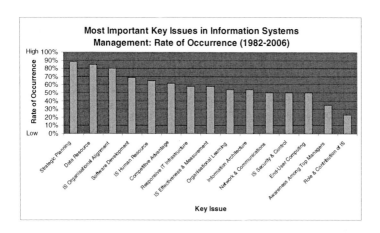

Appendix C

Figure 5: Perceived Most Important Key Issues in Information Systems Management - Median, Mode and Average Rank

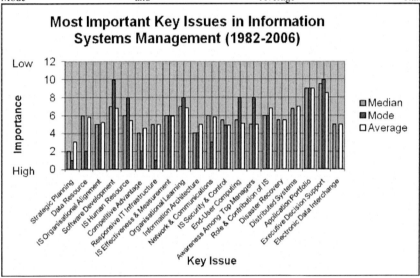

Integration of Booking Systems based on XML
Message Exchange

Alberto Guadalupi[1], Giuseppe Psaila[2]

[1] A.E.C. s.r.l.,
Piazza Pontida 7, I-24122, Bergamo, Italy,
e-mail: alberto@verticalbooking.com

[2] Università di Bergamo, Facoltà di Ingegneria,
Viale Marconi 5, I-24044 Dalmine (BG), Italy,
e-mail: psaila@unibg.it

Abstract. XML is recognized as the standard syntax to define communication protocols for e-commerce applications; messages exchanged by these protocols are based on an XML format. In particular, in the context of tourism, the *Open Travel Alliance* (OTA) [2] defined a very rich set of standard XML messages concerning e-business activities, like hotel booking, car rental, flight reservation, etc.; heterogeneous booking information systems can be part of a unique distributed tourism system that connects hotels, travel agencies, tour operators, Global Distribution System (GDS), Internet Distribution Systems (IDS) and travelers. The OTA standard is the most famous proposal, but several others are based on XML message exchange.

In this paper, we present a technique for integrating information systems with XML-based Message Exchange Services. The technique has been jointly developed by A.E.C. s.r.l., a young and dynamic Italian company working in the area of information systems for hotels and booking, and the Faculty of Engineering of the University of Bergamo. Moving from XML Schema specifications, the technique generates a mapping descriptions between the messages and the internal data structures of the information system. Then, two components named *Message Loader* and *Message Generator*, respectively load incoming messages and generate outcoming messages. As a result, the system is easily integrated with communication channels, and the correctness of XML message processing is guaranteed by the mapping information, directly derived from the XML Schema specifications.

1 Introduction

The wide use of XML-based formats to implement e-commerce solutions is a matter of fact. In several application fields, organizations are developing application-specific communication protocols based on the exchange of XML messages. In particular, an interesting effort has been done in the context of tourism, where the *Open Travel Alliance* (OTA) [2] defined a very rich set of standard XML messages concerning e-business activities, like hotel booking, car rental, flight reservation, etc.; relying on OTA messages, heterogeneous booking information systems can cooperate to provide tourists with an integrated and distributed booking system, where Global Distribution Systems (GDS), Internet Distribution Systems (IDS), and information systems of hotels, Tour Operators, and Travel Agencies can join their efforts to provide high quality travel and tourism services.

The OTA standard is just the most famous proposal, but in general developers of tourism information systems are choosing XML as the standard syntax for defining message exchange services. Thus, developers of information systems, in particular, in the field of tourism, have to face the problem of integrating their information systems with XML-based interfaces to other systems, both for incoming and outcoming messages.

The problem of effectively exploiting XML Schema specifications arose very early, after the definition of XML Schema. It appeared soon [7] that the integration of e-business processes had to heavily exploit XML-Schema Specifications.

Just a few years later, researchers tried to understand [12] if all potentials provided by XML Schema were exploited in practice. At that time, it was clear that much more work had to be done in the development of new solutions.

The main result of XML Schema adoption, is that a lot of (e-business) protocols are based on XML and messages are defined by means of XML Schema specifications. This makes necessary to easily (and possibly automatically) integrate systems and protocols in a unique framework. We found that the most famous effort is the *RosettaNet* project (see, for example, [9] [11]) where several techniques to enhance the integration of B2B processes were developed; however, they defined a set of standard messages that support a specific protocol; this protocols allows to share semantic information about the structure of actual B2B messages. Consequently, they do not have to deal with multiple XML Schema specifications.

A.E.C. s.r.l., a young and dynamic Italian company working in the area of information systems for hotels and booking, had to face the problem as well. To solve it in a flexible way, jointly developed, with the Faculty of Engineering of the University of Bergamo, a technique for integrating its booking information system with XML-based Message Exchange Services. Moving from a set of XML Schema specifications [10], that define the structure of exchanged messages, the integration technique is able to derive descriptions that allow to create a mapping between internal data structures and the elements in the XML Messages; then a component named *Message Loader* uses these mappings to actually map incoming XML messages into the internal representation, and a component named *Message Generator* maps the internal representation into the outcoming XML messages.

The result is a system that can be easily integrated with several IDS and external information systems, where the correctness of outcoming messages as well as the correctness of interpretation of incoming messages is guaranteed by the fact that mapping information is directly derived from the XML Schema specifications, that usually accompany XML-based standards. The paper will present the general ideas of the integration technique, showing its potential and effectiveness.

The paper is organized as follows. Section 2 presents the *Vertical Booking* system, within which the integration technique described in this paper was developed. Them Section 3 briefly introduces advanced features of XML Schema, that make hard to read and understand complex XML Schema specifications. Section 4 gives an overview of the OTA standard. Section 5 actually presents the software component named *Channel Manager*, that is based on the integration technique; the section also shows the architecture and how the integration technique works. Finally, Section 6 discusses the impact on business of the *Channel Manager* highlighting the main benefits obtained by its adoption, while Section 7 draws the conclusions.

2   The Vertical Booking System

A.E.C. srl has been involved in web-based development since 1999. In 2005 A.E.C. developed a booking engine for hotels named *Vertical Booking* [4]. The system fully assists the process of booking rooms, both from the hotel side and from the customer site; in particular, it provides the possibility of defining complex fare rules that dynamically change in time.

As Figure 1 shows, the system is based on the ASP (Application Service Provider) architecture. Hotel employee and/or hotel information systems are connected to the Vertical Booking System through the internet. On the other side, the system provides both a web interface for customers (people and enterprises) and a B2B interface to *channels*, such as GDS and IDS.

We recently addressed the need of integrating the system with several channels by developing the software called *Channel Manager*. The result is a system that provides hoteliers with a unique and simple interface to manage different IDS and GDS, with specific fares, booking rules and room inventories; all of that is based on one single room inventory, so that errors like overlapped reservations are avoided.

IDSs utilize a variety of formats for XML communication, possibly based on Open Travel Alliance (OTA) specifications, or on other continuously evolving formats. Therefore, the main design requirement we identified is that *Channel Manager* must be able to analyze XML schemas and to automatically read and generate XML messages based on the schemas.

More in details, the requirements are the following.

1. Ability to quickly create or modify XML interfaces to any kind of IDS partner.
2. Ability to manage different sets of XML schema specifications at the same time.
3. Ability to generate XML messages based on data extracted from within the database.

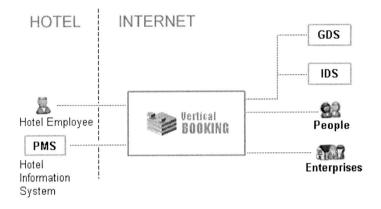

Fig. 1. The Vertical Booking System

4. Ability to read incoming XML messages and to store relevant application data into the database.

The result of the joint development with the Faculty of Engineering of the University of Bergamo, is a software (the *Channel Manager*) that can analyze complex XML schema specifications in few seconds, saving the structure of messages (described in a proprietary manner) into a specific database; this allows the creation of a mapping between internal data structures and the elements in the XML Messages.

The software includes a component named *Message Loader* that uses mapping information in the database to map incoming XML messages to the internal representation, and a component named *Message Generator* that maps the internal representation to the structure of outcoming XML messages.

Then, the *Channel Manager* can be interconnected (in a bidirectional way) with any kind of *Internet Distribution System*, providing hoteliers with an effective and integrated system to deal with several channels, avoiding long and repetitive updating operations giving a higher performance and security, if compared with systems based on screen scraping techniques.

At the moment, thanks to the *Channel Manager* software, the *Vertical Booking* system is connected with several IDS and GDS services, most of them based on OTA messages. Figure 2 shows their logos.

3 XML Schema

XML [6] provides a mean to define the structure of documents, named DTD (Document Type Definition). A DTD can be either part of the document itself, or external to the document and referenced by it; if a document complies with

Expedia.com
Hotels.com
Booking.com
Active Hotels
Venere.com
Hotel.de
ITWG
Ghrs Hotles
MV & Travel
HotelsChart.com
WorldBy.com
RatesToGo.com
HSR
SynXis
HotelREZ
Design Hotels

Fig. 2. Services Connected with the Vertical Booking System

a DTD, it is said *valid* for that DTD. Consequently, a DTD defines a class of documents.

Since the beginning, it appeared clear that a DTD presents some limitations and problems. First of all, the syntactic structure of a DTD is not homogeneous with the rest of the document. Second, the concept of *data type* for attributes is totally missing. Finally, DTDs are not compatible with the concept of *namespace* [5], that gives the possibility of freely integrating fragments belonging to different namespaces in the same document (see, for example, XSLT [8], the SOAP protocol [3], eb-XML [1]).

Moving from these considerations, in 2001 the World Wide Web Consortium (W^{3}C) defined XML Schema [10], aiming at overtaking the DTD limitations.

An XML Schema specification is an XML document defined in the namespace of XML Schema. Elements belonging to this namespace are prefixed by `xs:`. Let us briefly explain the main features provided by XML Schema.

```
    . . .
<!ELEMENT name (family,given,birthdate,email*)>
<!ELEMENT family (#PCDATA)>
<!ELEMENT given (#PCDATA)>
<!ELEMENT email (#PCDATA)>
<!ELEMENT birthdate (#PCDATA)>
<!ATTLIST employee salary CDATA #IMPLIED>
    . . .
```

Fig. 3. DTD fragment of a sample XML document.

```
..xmi  version  i.u  ..
<xs:schema xmlns:xs='http://www.w3.org/2001/XMLSchema'>
  . . .
 <xs:element name="employee">
  <xs:complexType>
   <xs:sequence>
    <xs:element ref="family"/>
    <xs:element ref="given"/>
    <xs:element ref="birthdate"/>
    <xs:element ref="email"
        minOccurs="0" minOccurs="unbounded"/>
   </xs:sequence>
  </xs:complexType>
  <xs:attribute name="salary" type="xs:integer"/>
 </xs:element>

 <xs:element name="family" type='xs:string'/>
 <xs:element name="given" type='xs:string'/>
 <xs:element name="birthdate" type='xs:date'/>
  . . .
```

Fig. 4. Fragment of XML-Schema specification, for the same documents described by DTD in Figure3.

- XML Schema constructs encompass all DTD constructs, even though they use a slightly different approach. In fact, for defining the structure of element contents, regular expression operators (allowed in DTDs) are not allowed in XML Schema: an element (defined by means of the construct xs:element) or a sequence of elements (defined with the construct xs:sequence) has two properties, named minOccurs and maxOccurs, that specify the minimum and maximum number of repetitions, respectively. Alternatives are specified by means of the xs:choice construct.
- XML Schema adds the concept of *data type*: attribute values are now typed strings, such as numbers, dates, etc..
- XML Schema moves toward concepts typical of object-orientation, by adding specific and novel constructs. By means of the construct xs:complexType it is possible to define new complex types, i.e., complex structures for element content and attributes; complex types can be used to define elements, or to define other complex types (incapsulation).
- Furthermore, the construct xs:extension is close to the concept of *inheritance*. By means of this construct, a new complex type can be defined as an extension of a previously defined complex type or element, by adding new attributes or extending the content structure.

We can notice that, by means of XML Schema, it is possible to write very complex specifications. If stressed, this possibility allows to obtain very well modularized specifications, where complex types are reused several times.

```
<employee salary="1500">
  <family>Smith</family>
  <given>John</given>
  <birthdate>1980-02-01</birthdate>
</employee>
. . .
```

Fig. 5. Fragment of a sample XML document defined by DTD in Figure 3 and XML-Schema specification in Figure 4.

However, for a person that has to read such specifications, the task of understanding the specification might become hard.

Figure 5 shows a fragment of an XML document: element `employee` describes data about an employee. Family name, given name, birthdate and a possibly empty (as in the fragment) list of e-mail addresses are described by specific elements, while the salary is described by attribute `salary`.

Note that both the DTD in Figure 3 and the XML-Schema specification in Figure 4 describe the same fragment. However, notice that XML-Schema is able to specify data types for attributes and contents (`xs:date` and `xs:integer`); in the DTD, both birthdate and salary are generic (non typed) strings.

Finally, notice that the XML-Schema specification is an XML document itself, where elements are prefixed by `xs:`, the prefix for XML-Schema elements.

4   The OTA Specification

In this section, we briefly introduce the main characteristics of the OTA specification. It is a complex specification, because it is designed to cover all travel and tourism e-commerce processes.

4.1   OTA Messages

OTA messages are designed to cover the overall spectrum of commercial transactions concerning travel and tourism. In fact, the goal is to support the integration of heterogeneous systems.

Consequently, the number of OTA messages is impressive: more than 240. They cover, but are not limited to, the following applications.

- *Flight Booking.* These messages covers transactions concerning flight booking and ticket purchase.
- *Rails.* These messages cover transactions concerning railway tickets and timetables.
- *Car Rental.* These messages can be exploited to integrate car rental services.
- *Hotel Booking.* These large set of messages covers room booking, fare definition, room availability checking, etc..

71

– *Package Tours/Holiday Booking*. This group of messages covers package tours selling and holiday booking.

Each message is defined by a specific XML Schema file. However, the specification is modular, since messages share several common structures and data types. Consequently, XML Schema files usually recursively include several other XML Schema files.

The result is that the complete set of XML Schema files for OTA messages is composed of several hundreds of files. It is clear that it is hard, for a human, to fully comprehend the structure of messages simply reading the XML Schema specifications; this task is hard also because OTA specifications heavily use complex types and inheritance. In contrast, an automatic analyzer can extract patterns and attributes that need to be filled in with application specific values. This is the idea behind the technique we are going to introduce in the remainder of the paper.

4.2 Protocols

The structure defined for OTA messages is, of course, independent of the communication protocol exploited to send messages. However, OTA specifications considers some standard solutions, based on well known protocols.

– *SOAP*. The *Simple Object Access Protocol* (SOAP) [3] is a standard communication protocol that can be used to realize complex interaction between information systems.

Mainly, SOAP defines an XML message called *envelop*, that is able to contain any kind of XML content. For this reason, OTA considers SOAP as a possible communication protocol to send OTA messages. In general, SOAP messages are sent by means of the HTTP or SMTP protocols.

– *ebXML*. *Electronic Business using eXtensible Markup Language* (ebXML) "is a modular suite of specifications that enables enterprises of any size and in any geographical location to conduct business over the Internet" [1].

In practice, ebXML is a framework that allows two commercial partners to exchange business messages in order to integrate their collaborative processes. While ebXML provides standard messages to look for new partners providing e-business interfaces, it does not provide any standard for application specific messages, but generic XML containers for sending messages. OTA defines application-specific messages, that can be sent by means of the ebXML communication services.

– *HTTP*. A simpler solution, that is usually adopted by IDS, is to exploit the *Hyper Text Transfer Protocol* to exchange OTA messages. The advantage of this solution is that the software layer necessary to implement the communication services are reduced, thus it is easier to implement the communication services.

However, the basic characteristic of HTTP, i.e., the fact that it is a *request/response* protocol, gives rise to two possible interaction models.

72

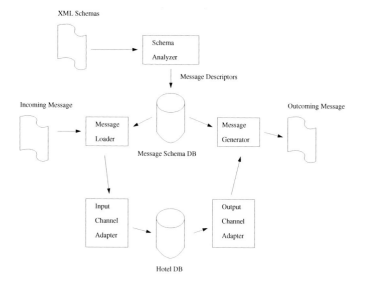

Fig. 6. Architecture of the Channel Manager

- *Push Model.* in this model, a system is active w.r.t. the interaction. Suppose that system S1 must send data about a reservation to system S2. Thus, S1 sends a HTTP request to S2, where the request contains all data about the reservation; within the HTTP response, S2 replies saying whether the reservation has been accepted or not.
- *Pull Model.* In this model, a system is passive w.r.t. the communication: it stores all data to communicate, and wait until the partner system asks to send pending data.

  For example, consider again systems S1 and S2. S1 collects data about reservations, that remain pending. When S2 is ready to receive reservations, asks S1 whether there are pending reservations, by sending a message in the HTTP request; S1 replies sending a message (in the HTTP response) containing the pending reservations. At this point, S2 sends a new message (in the HTTP request) by means of which it notifies the acceppted reservations; then S2 replies (with a message in the HTTP response) to acknowledges the transaction.

We can then observe that the push model requires one single HTTP session, while the pull model requires two HTTP sessions. In particular, the pull model requires two more messages to exchange: the OTA specifications provide messages for a variety of communication sessions based on both the two models; consequently, OTA defines an incredible number of messages (more than 200).

In this section, we describe the main features of the *Channel Manager*, the component that couples the *Vertical Booking* system with external systems.

The architecture of the *Channel Manager* is reported in Figure 6, and described below.

- The core of the *Channel Manager* is the *Message Schema DB*: it stores descriptions about messages to be used for a given channel. These descriptors are used both to load messages and to generate new messages.
- The *Hotel DB* is the database where data about room inventory and fare descriptions for a specific hotel managed by the *Vertical Booking* system are stored.
- The *Schema Analyzer* is the crucial component of the *Channel Manager*. When a new channel is created, it is run to analyze the new XML Schema definitions: it extracts *Schema Descriptors*, that are stored into the *Message Schema DB*, in order to create a mapping betwen internal data structures and messages.
- The *Message Loader* actually reads incoming messages and extracts relevant data, that must be stored into the *Hotel DB*. Based on the tree structure of the document and by exploiting mapping information associated with schema descriptors, it generates an intermediate data structure, that represents the tree structure of the document in an abstract way. This intermediate data structure is passed to the *Input Channel Adapter*.
- The *Input Channel Adapter* has the responsibility of dealing with the specific channel. First of all, this means that it actually extracts data from the intermediate data structure; then, it must actually drives the interaction (communication sessions are based on the bidirectional exchange of several messages) with the external system, as far as the incoming messages are concerned; finally, it stores data about the current transaction into the *Hotel DB*.
- The *Output Channel Adapter* plays the dual role of the *Input Channel Adapter*. It drives the interaction with the external system, as far as the outcoming messages are concerned; similarly to the dual component, it accesses the *Hotel DB* to obtain data about the active transactions. It generates an intermediate data structure that is sent to the *Message Generator*.
- The *Message Generator* receives the intermediate data structure containing data to send to the external system; then, based on the *Message Descriptors* that describe the message to generate and the associated mapping information, it actually generates the XML message to send.

We observe that the components that directly face with XML (*Schema Analyzer*, *Message Loader* and *Message Generator*) are independent of the particular communication protocol and message structure. In contrast, the *Input Channel Adapter* and the *Output Channel Adapter* are strongly dependent on protocols and message contents.

We obtained a loose integration, because only the two latter components are dependent on the channel. However, thanks to the fact that they do not have to directly read or generate XML messages, they are independent of their actual lexical and syntactic features. The programmer that implements the adapter can concentrate only on the protocol and the execution of transactions.

The result is that the addition of new channels to the system is performed in a very fast way, with the advantage that the correctness of both incoming and otcoming messages (and their compliance with standards) is ensured by the *Message Loader* and the *Message Generator*.

5.1 The Schema Analyzer

This component of the *Channel Manager* analyzes the schemas of messages and produces, for each message, a set of descriptors that are stored into the *Schema DB*. Let us understand how the *Schema Analyzer* works.

- First of all, the *Schema Analyzer* reads the XML Schema specification files involved in the definition of a specific message. It extracts information about elements, attributes, types (elementary or complex) and content structures.
- Second, the *Schema Analyzer* resolves references to complex types (elements whose structure is defined by a complex type); then, it resolves inheritance of complex types or elements (the `xs:extension` construct provided by XML Schema).
- At this point, the *Schema Analyzer* can build the full set of parent-child relationships. At this stage, it also recognizes complex nested occurrences of `xs:choice` and `xs:sequence`, possibly obtained by references to complex types or by occurrences of the `xs:extension` construct. This work is essential, in order to understand the actual structure of element contents.
- Finally, the *Schema Analyzer* identifies *relevant sub-paths*. These describes fragments of tree rooted in *key points*.
  A *key point* is a point where the structure of the tree can change, depending on the data represented in the document. Thus, key points are occurrences of the `xs:choice` construct or occurrences of the `xs:sequence` construct with variable number of repetitions.

The set of descriptors obtained at the end of this process is stored into the *Message Schema DB*. Then, a suitable user interface provided to the programmer allows to define *labels* for all those items in the message that carry application information, i.e., element attributes and content of elements containing only (possibly typed) text. We call these items *relevant application data items*.

5.2 The Message Loader

When an incoming message is processed, this component actually reads the message and, based on the information stored in the *Schema DB*, builds the intermediate representation of the document. In particular, the intermediate representation is an abstract tree, where each relevant application data item is extracted from the document and labeled with the associated label. The analysis of the incoming message is driven by descriptors present in the *Message Schema DB*: in fact, it must navigate the tree representation of the message, identify relevant application data items, identify key points: a key point causes the insertion of a new nesting level in the intermediate representation.

Then the abstract tree is passed to the *Input Channel Adapter*: it navigates the abstract tree and, based on labels associated to relevant application data items, it is able to match extracted data items with internal variables and tables in the *Hotel DB*. Note that the programmer has to focus on semantic aspects of the document, that are key points and labels; if labels are properly defined, in order to give a precise semantics to each relevant application data item, it is really easy for the programmer to extract data items from the abstract tree.

5.3   The Message Generator

The *Message Generator* does the opposite work, i.e., it generates the outcoming messages. It receives the abstract tree from the *Output Channel Adapter*.

Similarly to what we said for the *Message Loader*, the programmer that implements the *Output Channel Adapter* must focus only on semantic aspects of the outcoming message. He/she must take care of *key points* and labels of relevant application data items; the implementation maps internal data (in main memory data structures or tables in the *Hotel DB*) into the abstract tree. Then, it passes the abstract tree to the *Message Generator*.

Based on the schema descriptors present in the *Message Schema DB*, the *Message Generator* generates the actual XML structure of the message. In particular, it is driven by the presence of key points in the abstract tree, that are used to decide what to generate in case of alternatives (the `xs:choice` construct) or repetition of sequences. Furthermore, when the *Message Generator* finds a relevant application data item to insert into the message, it identifies its value in the abstract tree by means of the label (it looks for the label in the current nesting level of the abstract tree).

6   Impact on Business

After the technical discussion, it is time to duscuss about the impact on business, that we observed after the introduction of the *Channel Manager*.

First of all, we have to consider the effect on the creation on new channels in the *Vertical Booking* system. The *Channel Manager* proved to be quite effective. A.E.C.'s programmers programmers report that they easily comprehend the structure of messages, even when their structure is very complex. Then, they are able to easily give a semantic characterization to relevant data items. Finally, they confirm that the implementation effort is limited, and focused on the key aspects of the integration.

Thus, the level of productivity in developing new channels is very high. In Section 2, and in Figure 2 in particular, we show the services currently integrated with the *Vertical Booking* system: the integration of all these services took only less than one year.

Furthermore, channels are reliable, because the interface with channels is rigorously based on official XML-Schema specifications[3].

If we consider the impact on business in terms of revenue, we can consider both the hoteller point of view, and A.E.C. point of view.

From the hotellers point of view, the integration of the *Vertical Booking* system, on which they rely for managing room booking, with IDS and GDS gave an immediate revenue. Many small hotels that originally worked mainly in a local market, after the interconnection with IDS and GDS rapidly increased the number of customers coming from foreign countries, but the number of Italian customers significantly increased as well. The reason is that the integration with IDS and GDS strongly improved their visibility to customers that use web portals to book hotels and organize their trips.

From the point of view of A.E.C., the fast integration process made possible by the *Channel Manager*, allowed to better meet hotellers requests, by providing a large number of interconnected IDS and GDS in a short time. The result is a better service for hotellers, that can obtain higher revenue from their activity. As a result, this means higher productivity in the development of services (lower cost of development), satisfied hotellers and new hotels that adopt the *Vertical Booking* system.

To conclude our discussion, we can say that the availability of a new communication technology for e-business certainly opens new interesting business opportunities, but also creates new technical challenges and obstacles that may strongly limit the effective adoption of the new technology (and, at the end, reduce the business opportunities, especially for small enterprise). The experience described in this paper clearly shows that only the development of innovative techniques to manage new technologies can give the possibility to actually take advantage by them.

7   Conclusions

In this paper, we presented the experience in the development of *Channel Manager*, the software component for integrating the *Vertical Booking* system, developed by A.E.C., with external channels (GDS and IDS).

The development of the *Channel Manager* was based on the main requirement that the integration with external systems had to be loose, in order to strongly reduce the cost of development of interfaces to channels, based on XML messages.

---

[3] During the integration with an IDS, the *Channel Manager* detected not compliant messages erroneously sent by the IDS; this bug were signaled to and promptly fixed by the owner of the IDS.

To achieve the goal, the *Channel Manager* analyzes the XML Schema specifications of messages, extracting descriptors that are stored into its database; the programmer adds labels that semantically characterizes application data items. Then, incoming messages are loaded and application data items are extracted and represented in an internal data structure; outcoming messages are generated moving from the same data structure; both tasks are based on message descriptors stored in the database. The consequence is that the actual interface to the channel simply has either to read or to generate the intermediate data structure, by exploiting labels. No knowledge about the actual and detailed structure of XML messages is needed.

The impact on business is significant, both in terms of productivity in the development of services, and in terms of new market opportunities open fo hotellers by the world wide visibility ensured by IDS, GDS and travel portals.

References

1. *Electronic Business using eXtensible Markup Language.* UN/CEFACT, OASIS, http://www.ebxml.org/.
2. *Open Travel Agency (OTA).* Open Travel Alliance, http://www.opentravel.org/.
3. SOAP 1.2 SPecifications. Technical report, World Wide Web Consortium, http://www.w3.org/.
4. *Vertical Booking.* A.E.C: s.r.l., http://www.verticalbooking.com/.
5. T. Bray, D. Hollander, and A. Layman. Namespaces in XML. Technical Report REC-xml-names-19990114, World Wide Web Consortium, http://www.w3.org/TR/1999/REC-xml-names-19990114/, January 1999.
6. T. Bray, J. Paoli, and C. M. Sperberg-McQueen. Extensible markup language (XML). Technical Report PR-xml-971208, World Wide Web Consortium, December 1997.
7. C. Bussler. B2B protocol standards and their role in semantic B2B integration engines. *IEEE Data Engineering Bulletin*, 24(1):58–63, 2001.
8. J. Clark. XSL transformations (XSLT - version 1.0. Technical Report REC-xslt-19991116, World Wide Web Consortium, 1999.
9. S. Damodaran. B2B integration over the internet with XML rosettanet successes and challenges. In *13th international World Wide Web conference*, pages 188 – 195, New York, NY, USA, 2004.
10. H: S. Thompson, D. Beech, M. Maloney, and N. Mendelsohn. XML schema part 1: Structures. Technical Report REC-xmlschema-1-20010502, World Wide Web Consortium, http://www.w3.org/TR/2001/REC-xmlschema-1-20010502/, May 2001.
11. J. Tikkala, P. Kotinurmi, and T. Soininen. Implementing a RosettaNet business-to-business integration platform using J2EE and Web services. In *Seventh IEEE International Conference on E-Commerce Technology, CEC 2005*, pages 553 – 558, Munich, Germany, 2005.
12. F. Dorloff V. Schmitz, J. Leukel. Does B2B data exchange tap the full potential of XML schema languages ? In *16-th Bled eCommerce Conference eTransformation*, Bled, Slovenia,, 2003.

Innovation and Competition in Payment Systems

Armando Calabrese[1], Massimo Gastaldi[2], Irene Iacovelli[1], and Nathan Levialdi Ghiron[1]

[1]Department of Enterprise Engineering, University of Rome 'Tor Vergata', Viale del Politecnico 1, 00133 Rome, Italy
[2]Department of Electrical and Information Engineering, University of "L'Aquila", Monteluco di Roio, 67100 L'Aquila, Italy
Corresponding Author: iacovelli@disp.uniroma2.it

Abstract. This paper proposes a model which analyses the role of technological innovation in the competitiveness and efficiency of the payment system industry. The performance of this industry is described through the use of a mathematical model and the strategies of platforms are analysed considering the role of technological innovation. The paper shows how technological development is the most common competitive strategy in an oligopolistic market of payment platforms. Moreover, the paper shows that these platforms can develop product/service innovations or price differentiations in order to deal with market competition effectively.

Keywords: Two-sided markets, payment systems, technological innovation, business innovation.

1 Introduction

Over the last few years, payment systems have been characterised by several technological innovations, by a growing competition among the intermediaries traditionally involved in the sector, and also by competition between these intermediaries and telecommunications companies.

It is possible to differentiate between incremental and radical innovations. An incremental innovation involves small technological changes, thus the existing products are able to remain competitive in the market; a radical innovation, on the other hand, involves sizeable technological developments, thus the existing products cease to be competitive in the market and are rendered obsolete. In the case of incremental innovations, incumbents can use their resources and knowledge in order to leverage the technology development; while in the case of radical innovations, new entrants may have a significant competitive advantage as they need not change their resources and know-how. Furthermore, from a strategic standpoint, incumbents may have no incentive to invest in the innovation if, by doing so, they might run the risk of cannibalising their existing products.

Radical innovations in the payment industry have presented challenges to the market players and instigated major transformations. Such innovations are now taking place throughout the world. In the USA, for instance, a system based on fingerprint recognition, Pay By Touch (www.paybytouch.com), has been developed. Incremental innovations are emerging even more rapidly. In Japan, for example, DoCoMo (www.nttdocomo.com) has developed a smart-card integrated into the 3G mobile phone network in order to allow users to make payments and carry out financial transactions [1]. In addition, credit card compagnie have introduced 'contactless' technology.

The aim of this paper is to analyse the role of technological innovation in the competitiveness and efficiency of payment system services. More specifically we have extended the Chakravorti and Roson model [2] in order to study the competition among three payment networks, each one characterised by different technologies. In fact, the development of technological innovation allows the entry of new players into the market and changes the competition for traditional incumbents. Thus we consider the competition among three players – the *incumbent* (the traditional credit card system) and *new entrants* (two telecommunications companies who, thanks to innovations, may now enter the payment market) – in order to represent and analyse the present payment system industry, characterised by two main technologies (mobile and biometric) competing with the traditional credit card technology.

The paper is organised as follows: in section 2 we define a two-sided market, highlighting the main contributions of the literature and the main differences with respect to the model proposed. In section 3 we describe the players in the present payment system industry. Section 4 introduces the model while in section 5 we analyse the strategic interaction between platforms. In section 6 we conclude the paper with some observations and comments.

2 Literature Review

Payment system services are regarded as *two-sided markets*, in so far as their operation depends on the combination of preferences of two different clusters of users: consumers and merchants ([3]; [4]; [5]; [6]; [7];[8], and [9]). Evans[10] states that the interaction between these categories of users is influenced by the presence of *indirect network-effects*: the benefit for consumers of joining a platform depends on the number of merchants who accept the cards, whilst the benefit of joining a platform for merchants is related to how the cards are used by consumers.Thus the opposite network size represents a quality parameter in the platform adoption [9]; and since the network size depends on its price, the utility for a card user depends on both market prices [9]. Furthermore, according to Wright [11] and [12], such an interaction between the two market sides of a platform depends on the strategies which that particular platform chooses.

Many authors have studied competition among payment instruments ([13]; [14];[15];[16];[17]; [18]; and [19]). In particular, Chakravorti and Roson [2] construct a model to study competing payment networks offering differentiated products in terms of benefits to consumers and merchants. They analyse market equilibrium in several market structures: duopolistic competition and cartels, symmetric and asymmetric networks, taking into consideration alternative assumptions about consumer preferences in both cases. Their results show how competition increases consumer and merchant welfare.

The model proposed in the paper differs from the existing literature. Firstly, it focuses on the relationship between innovation and platform competition, while this topic has received little attention from the literature ([20]; [21];and [22]). The paper evaluates the role that technology innovation has in the competitiveness and efficiency of the payment system industry and analyses whether innovation represents a threat or an opportunity for such an industry. Moreover, there is evidence that payment platforms can develop product/service innovations or price differentiations in order to deal with market competition effectively [23].

Secondly, we extend the Chakravorti and Roson [2] model of duopolistic competition to three players in order to study the effects produced in the market by three dominant innovations (contactless cards, mobile phones and biometric payment systems). In fact, due to the *Sepa* (Single euro payments area) project, which aims to realise an integrated market of retail payments by 2010, the technological development has been increasing the number of payment devices: new market opportunities will be available both to the incumbent (traditional credit card operators) and to the new entrants (telecommunication firms and large distribution networks). Thus it is useful to extend the Chakravorti and Roson [2] model from two to three competitors in order to analyse the market development due to both market agreements (Sepa) and technological innovations.

Thirdly, the paper describes the pricing policy of payment systems according to different strategies of technological innovation.

3 The Market Players in the Payment Systems

In recent years, the traditional credit card industry has been threatened by technological developments which have emerged throughout the world and have resulted in tremendous transformations in the sector. At present the biometric and cellular telephone payment systems are the most innovative technologies and also the most used by both consumers and merchants.

Pay By Touch (www.paybytouch.com) has created a biometric payment system based on fingerprint recognition. The mechanism used is rather simple: at the check-out of a shop the consumer places his/her finger on a scanner. After the customer has to enter a secret code number and the purchase will immediately be debited from his/her bank account.

DoCoMo (www.nttdocomo.com) has developed a smart-card integrated into the 3G mobile phone network in order to allow users to carry out financial transactions. The *contactless* communication between an electronic reader and the chip inside the mobile telephone is activated by means of electromagnetic waves. When greater sums of money are concerned, the customer is required to enter a PIN for identification.

Credit card companies have also introduced cards with *contactless* technology. The consumer holds the card or payment device in front of the Point of Sale (POS) terminal, sending the payment information to a special reader which carries out the transaction.

The attitudes of consumers and merchants towards adopting and accepting an innovative payment system normally show some resistance to change. We can assume that any innovation in a payment system will be more easily adopted if the potential consumers and merchants perceive it as being advantageous in terms of:

- *learning costs*: the necessary time spent and the difficulties involved in order to learn how to use the new technologies;
- *security*: a guarantee against the possibility of fraud;
- *speed*: the time required to carry out an economic transaction;
- *interoperability*: the degree of compatibility with respect to other similar systems.

In this paper each platform is given a value between 0 and 1 for each of the attributes listed above, in order to calculate the maximum benefit of each consumer, τ, and the maximum benefit of each merchant, μ. The values τ and μ are the sums of each attribute, so they can have a value between 0 and 4. In fact, it is possible to assume that the lower the learning costs, the more widespread the innovation. Moreover, the greater the security and speed of an innovation in a payment system, the more widespread it will be. Lastly, it is possible to assume that the interoperability of a payment system facilitates its use in the markets.

4 The Model

The model describes the competition among four payment systems. Let us assume platform 1 represents the incumbent, i.e., the traditional credit card system (cards with a magnetic strip); platforms 2 and 3 represent the new entrants, the biometric and the RFID cellular phone systems respectively. The fourth system, which is not a technological platform at all, is cash. The latter is available to all consumers and merchants and does not require any additional fees; we suppose no utility is obtained by either consumers or merchants in using cash.

We adopt the main assumptions made by Chakravorti and Roson [2] model:
1. All consumers adopt a single payment system (singlehoming).
2. The total benefit that each consumer obtains by utilising the platform $i=1,2,3$ is given by multiplying the transaction benefit, h_i^c, by the number of merchants, D_i^m. The benefits, h_i^c, are distributed according a uniform distribution in $[0, \tau_i]$, where τ_i represents the maximum benefit that a consumer may obtain from platform i and is calculated by adding the different attributes together (learning costs, security, speed and interoperability).
3. Each consumer pays the platform an annual fee, f_i^c.
4. The consumer utility U^c (in using one of the three platforms) is calculated from the difference between total transaction benefits and fees. Moreover, let us assume that once a consumer becomes a member of a platform, he/she will use this payment system exclusively; thus the utility for the representative consumer U^c can be expressed as:

$$U^c = \max \{0, (h_1^c \, D_1^m - f_1^c), (h_2^c \, D_2^m - f_2^c), (h_3^c \, D_3^m - f_3^c)\} \ . \tag{1}$$

5. Each merchant sells only one product and is multi-homing; he pays each platform he uses a transaction fee, f_i^m.
6. The transaction benefit, h_i^m, which each merchant obtains from platform i, is distributed according a uniform distribution in $[0,\mu_i]$, where μ_i represents the maximum merchant benefit. μ_i is calculated by adding the different attributes together (learning costs, security, speed and interoperability).
7. The merchant utility U^m in using platform i is calculated from the difference between benefits and fees. A merchant will use a payment system if he obtains positive benefit from it; thus the utility for the representative merchant U^m can be expressed as:

$$U^m= \max\{0,(h_1^m\text{-}f_1^m)D_1^c\}+\max\{0,(h_2^m\text{-}f_2^m)D_2^c\}+\max\{0,(h_3^m\text{-}f_3^m)D_3^c\} \; . \qquad (2)$$

where D_i^c represents the number of consumers using the payment system offered by platform i.

A consumer utilises an alternative payment system to cash if such a system meets two requirements: it produces a positive utility and the consumer utility (U^c) – from the payment system chosen – is greater than for any other payment system.

We use the same assumptions as the Chakravorti and Roson [2] model, but expand on them in order to encompass competition between the three platforms. The market share can be seen in Figure 1, where each consumer is represented by a point whose coordinates $(h_1^c D_1^m, h_2^c D_2^m, h_3^c D_3^m)$ express the total benefits of using platforms 1, 2 or 3 [each point is obtained by multiplying the three transaction benefits h_i^c by the number of merchants who accept the payment system i, D_i^m].

In Figure 1, the parallelepiped is divided into 8 sections. Each one is derived from the intersection of the parallelepiped with the three planes that are obtained according to the values assumed by f_i^c. Consumers within section 1 use cash, since the net benefits offered by the three platforms are negative. In sections 5, 2 and 4 consumers choose the system which offers them positive utility – the credit card system, the biometric system, and the cell phone system respectively. In sections 6, 8, and 3 the competition is only between the two platforms that offer a positive net benefit. In Figure 2, we show section 6 of parallelepiped (of Figure 1) where, in this particular case, the competition is between platform 1 (the credit card system) and 2 (the biometric system). In fact in section 6 since $h_1^c D_1^m > f_1^c$ and $h_2^c D_2^m > f_2^c$, the credit card system (platform 1) and the biometric system (platform 2) offer positive net benefits; while given that $h_3^c D_3^m < f_3^c$, mobile phone system (platform 3) offers a negative net benefit to customer. Figure 2 shows a volume divided into two parts. The grey section represents the percentage of demand equally divided between two platforms. In fact, if platforms offer consumers the same value of net benefits (grey volume of Figure 2), consumers choose on the basis of relative utility and the border between the two market shares is given by a 45 degree plane that splits the grey volume into two sections [2]. The white volume represents the additional percentage of demand to be added to the platform which offers the greatest net benefit to the consumer."Only the network offering the highest consumer surplus $(\tau D^m\text{-}f^c)$ attracts consumers" in the white volume [2]; for example if $(\tau_2 D_2^m\text{-}f_2^c) > (\tau_1 D_1^m\text{-}f_1^c)$ the consumer utility is the greatest using platform 2.

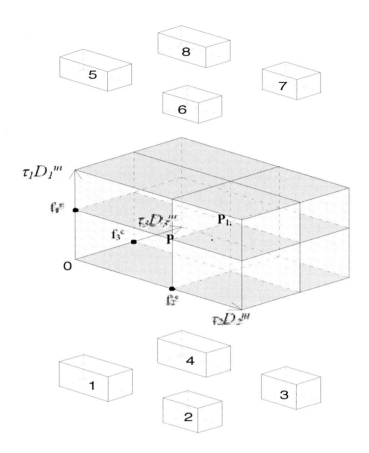

Fig. 1. Consumer market shares on platform i.

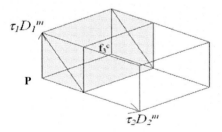

Fig. 2. Enlargement of section 6 of the parallelepiped in Figure 1

84

Section 7 represents the only volume in which consumers obtain positive utility in using all three platforms. The market share of each platform is represented in Figure 3. The white cube at the bottom left of Figure 3 is obtained by the third power of the minimum among $\tau_1 D_1{}^m\text{-}f_1{}^c$, $\tau_2 D_2{}^m\text{-}f_2{}^c$ and $\tau_3 D_3{}^m\text{-}f_3{}^c$, that is, the utility of the payment system which provides the minimum net benefit among all platforms. Since each platform provides a positive utility, each platform gains 1/3 of the white cube. In order to obtain the grey volume in Figure 3, we found the intermediate value among $\tau_1 D_1{}^m\text{-}f_1{}^c$, $\tau_2 D_2{}^m\text{-}f_2{}^c$ and $\tau_3 D_3{}^m\text{-}f_3{}^c$. The two platforms that offer the greatest net benefits gain half of the grey volume to sum to their respective market shares. In order to obtain the white parallelepiped at the right of Figure 3, we calculated the maximum among $\tau_1 D_1{}^m\text{-}f_1{}^c$, $\tau_2 D_2{}^m\text{-}f_2{}^c$ and $\tau_3 D_3{}^m\text{-}f_3{}^c$; then we calculated the volume of this parallelepiped. Only the platform that provides the maximum value of net benefit gains the additional market share represented by this parallelepiped.

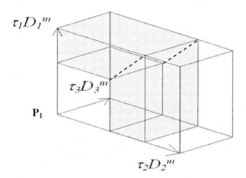

Fig. 3. Enlargement of section 7 of the parallelepiped in Figure 1

The market shares of consumer demand, for each platform, are obtained by adding the volumes (2,3,4,5,6,7,8) in Figure 1, divided by the total market demand ($m_1 * m_2 * m_3$). The total customer demand for each platform is represented respectively by the following Equations (3):

$$D_1^c = \{\{[b_1 * f_2^c * f_3^c] + [((\min(b_1,b_2))^2 * f_3^c \tfrac{1}{2}) + (b_1-(\min(b_1,b_2))) *((\min(b_1,b_2)) * f_3^c)] +$$
$$+ [((\min(b_1,b_3))^2 * f_2^c \tfrac{1}{2}) + (b_1-(\min(b_1,b_3))) *(\min(b_1,b_3)) * f_2^c] + Z_i\} / m_1 * m_2 * m_3\} * C$$

$$D_2^c = \{\{[b_2 * f_1^c * f_3^c] + [((\min(b_1,b_2))^2 * f_3^c \tfrac{1}{2}) + (b_2-(\min(b_1,b_2))) *((\min(b_1,b_2)) * f_3^c)] +$$
$$+ [((\min(b_2,b_3))^2 * f_1^c \tfrac{1}{2}) + (b_2-(\min(b_2,b_3))) *(\min(b_2,b_3)) * f_1^c] + Z_i\} / m_1 * m_2 * m_3\} * C$$

$$D_3^c = \{\{[b_3 * f_1^c * f_2^c] + [((\min(b_1,b_3))^2 * f_2^c \tfrac{1}{2}) + (b_3-(\min(b_1,b_3))) *((\min(b_1,b_3)) * f_2^c)] +$$
$$+ [((\min(b_2,b_3))^2 * f_1^c \tfrac{1}{2}) + (b_3-(\min(b_2,b_3))) *(\min(b_2,b_3)) * f_1^c] + Z_i\} / m_1 * m_2 * m_3\} * C$$

where:

$m_i = \tau_i * D_i^m$ $\forall i = 1,2,3;$

$b_i = m_i - f_i^c$ $\forall i = 1,2,3;$

C = total number of consumers;

$B = \min\{b_1, b_2, b_3\}; A = \max\{b_1, b_2, b_3\}; M = \max\{\min\{b_1, b_2\}; \min\{b_1, b_3\}; \min\{b_2, b_3\}\};$

$$
Z_i = \begin{cases}
\dfrac{B^3}{3} & \text{if the platform "i" produces net benefits lower than the other platforms;} \\[2em]
\dfrac{B^3}{3} + \dfrac{M^2 * B - B^3}{2} & \text{if the platform "i" produces net benefits between the ones produced by other platforms;} \\[2em]
\dfrac{B^3}{3} + \dfrac{M^2 * B - B^3}{2} + (A - M) * M * B & \text{if the platform "i" produces net benefits greater than other platforms.}
\end{cases}
$$

B^3 represents the white cube in the left of parallelepiped of Figure 3: according to Equation (3) for each platform, $1/3 * B^3$ has to be added to market shares. $M^2 * B - B^3$ represents the grey area in Figure 3: according to Equation (3) for two platforms that offer the greatest net benefits, $1/2 * (M^2 * B - B^3)$ has to be added to $1/3 * B^3$. $(A - M) * M * B$ represents the white volume on the right part of parallelepiped of Figure 3: according to Equation (3) for the platform that provide maximum net benefits $(A - M) * M * B$ has to be added to $1/3 * B^3 + 1/2 * (M^2 * B - B^3)$.

Under the assumption that the merchants accept the payment system i if and only if the benefits are greater than the costs $(h_i^m \geq f_i^m)$, the demand of the merchants is equal to:

$$
D_i^m = Pr(h_i^m \geq f_i^m) * M = (1 - K_i^m (f_i^m)) * M . \tag{4}
$$

where M represents the number of merchants on the market.

For simplicity, let us assume that the merchants benefits are distributed with a uniform distribution, K_i^m, in $[0, \mu_i]$.

Each platform faces two types of costs: the annual cost, g_i, for serving a consumer and a transaction cost, c_i, for serving a merchant.

The profit of each platform is given by:

$$
\pi_i = (f_i^c - g_i) \, D_i^c + (f_i^m - c_i) \, D_i^m \, D_i^c . \tag{5}
$$

The platforms choose the fees of consumers and merchants simultaneously and not cooperatively in order to maximise their profits.

The results obtained are equivalent to those of Chakravorti and Roson [2], i.e., the fees that maximise profits are determined by a modified Lerner's index:

$$p^c + f^m - c = (p^c / \varepsilon^c) = [f^m / (\varepsilon^m + \varepsilon^{cm} - \varepsilon^m \varepsilon^c)] \ . \tag{6}$$

where $p^c = (f^c - g)/D^m$ "is the per-transaction revenue minus cost from serving a consumer" [2].

For simplicity, let us suppose that both elasticity of the consumer's demand, ε^c, and elasticity of the merchant's demand, ε^m, are: for the consumer $\varepsilon^c = 1/\tau$ and for the merchant $\varepsilon^m = 1/\mu$. Thus, if the benefit τ for the consumer and the benefit μ for the merchant increase, each market side is not particularly sensitive to price variation. As regards the elasticity, ε^{cm} (variation of the consumers' demand with respect to a variation of the merchants' fee), let us suppose that it is directly proportional to $1/\mu$, multiplied by a constant $\lambda = 0.8$. In fact, the lower the platform sets merchant fees, the more the merchant demand increases and, indirectly, the more the consumer demand increases.

5 The Simulation: Innovation and Competitive Strategies

In this section we analyse the competition between the *incumbent* (the traditional credit card system) and the *new entrants* (the biometric and the cell phone systems). In order to do this we will employ some numerical simulations whose data have been tested through interviews with experts on such technologies and industries. The simulations will be determined through the use of *Matlab (MATrix LABoratory)* software; they are based on the following assumptions:

1. The three platforms choose their strategies simultaneously and not cooperatively and each platform has a consumer demand as defined by Equation (3). The demand of each payment system depends both on the net benefit of the system itself and on the net benefit generated by the competitors.
2. Expert opinion suggests that the annual cost, g_i, for serving a consumer and the transaction cost, c_i, for serving a merchant may be represented by utilizing the following values:

Table 1. Platforms costs on the consumers' side, g_i and on the merchants' side, c_i

Costs	Credit card system	Biometric system	Cell phone system
g_i	1	0.8	1.1
c_i	0.6	1.4	0.9

3. Using the attributes described in section 3 and according to interviews with experts on such technologies and industries, we calculated the maximum consumer benefit, τ, and merchant benefit, μ, for each platform.

Table 2. Consumer benefits and merchant benefits

Benefits	Credit card system	Biometric system	Cell phone system
τ	1.2	3.5	2.5
μ	1.6	3.5	3

4. In our analysis we fixed the merchant fee, f_i^m, and according to Equation (6), we obtained the customer fee, f_i^c.
5. Furthermore, we assumed that the incumbent can choose between two options: *proactive* and *reactive*. The proactive strategy consists of an investment in technology and it leads to an improvement in benefits (if compared to Table 2) both on the consumers' side, τ, and on the merchants' side, μ. The reactive strategy, which is a passive approach to innovation, does not involve any investment in technologies and consequently does not generate any change in benefits (if compared to Table 2).

    New entrants have to decide between a proactive or reactive strategy too.
6. Should the three platforms choose a reactive strategy, the merchant fees, f_i^m, will be greater than the costs on the merchant side, c_i. So according to the interviews with experts:

$$f_i^m = c_i + 0.2 \ . \qquad (7)$$

  where 0.2 is a mark-up for each transaction.

7. Should platform i choose a reactive strategy and at least one of the rival platforms a proactive one, we assume that platform i will reduce the merchant fee by 0.1 [if compared to Equation (7)] in order to be competitive in the market. Finally, if a platform opts for a proactive strategy, the merchant fee will rise by 0.2 [if compared to Equation (7)] since the innovation involves the installation of new POS. Thus according to Equation (6) the merchant fee (f_i^m) variation will cause a customer fee (f_i^c) variation.
8. Following Chakravorti and Roson [2], we also consider the market shares in our simulations. The platform profits are calculated according to Equation (5).

   According to the simulation employed we found that proactive strategies for all three platforms determine a Nash equilibrium; according to the experts interviewed and market analyses it represents the current dynamics of the payment systems industry. In fact, over the last few years it has been characterised by incremental and radical innovations and by the entry of competitors traditionally from other industrial sectors (i.e. telecommunications) into the market. For the incumbents (traditional credit cards operators), these new players represent a threat and stimulate innovation in order to compete in the market effectively.

   Moreover employing other simulations and changing the data inputs, we analysed the relationship between technological development and platform fees, their demands and their profits. As far as the relationship between benefit and fee is concerned, it is clear that an increase in benefit implies an increase in both fixed costs and variable costs, and that this is reflected on the fees increase. Whereas regarding the relationship between benefit and demand functions and between benefit and profit, in the case a platform increases its level of net provided benefits, both the consumers and the merchants will opt for such a system; thus the platforms will increase their respective market share and consequently their profits.

Moreover, there exist a threshold value of technological benefit – 3.5 for consumers and 3 for merchants – above which the consumers or merchants become 'saturated' and are not affected by technology improvements. In fact, above these values (3.5 and 3) if a player decides to adopt a reactive strategy (that is it decides not to innovate) while the rivals a proactive one (that is they decide to innovate), there will not be a drop in the market share of platform characterised by a reactive strategy.

We observed that both the consumers and the merchants mostly utilize and accept the credit card system, then the cell phone system, and lastly the biometric system. This is due to the fact that both the consumers' and the merchants' attitude towards the adoption and acceptance of an innovative payment system normally shows a certain degree of idiosyncrasy.

Regarding pricing structure, it was observed that in 85% of cases the platforms charged lower prices on the side of the platform that creates strong network externalities on the other side of the market.

6 Conclusions

In this paper we showed how an oligopolistic competition in the payment system industry will make the platforms to improve customer and merchant benefits. This result demonstrates that in a payment oligopoly, innovation may be one of the main competitive strategies for market players. Indeed, in such industries the payment platforms must develop products and services in order to remain competitive in the market [24].

Moreover we noticed that investment in technology both on the side of the consumers, τ, and on the side of the merchants, μ, has consequences which affect the demand of the consumers and of the merchants; the profits of the platform; the consumer fee, and lastly the merchant fee. In fact it was found that these variables increase with the increase of benefit offered and so with the degree of innovation generated.

References

1. Hagiu, A:I-modes and Octopi: will Asia Reshape the World's Payment Industry?, Market Platform Dynamics, report:0613, (2006)
2. Chakravorti, S. and Roson, R.: Platform Competition in Two-Sided Markets: The Case of Payment Networks, Review of Network Economics, vol 5, pp.118-142, (2006)
3. Armstrong, M: Competition in Two-Sided Markets, mimeo, University College London, (2004)
4. Calabrese A., Gastaldi, M., and Levialdi Ghiron, N: Development Prospects for Mobile Networks: the Multi-sided Platform Approach in the Competition Analysis, "in Cooper R., Lloyd A., Madden G., Schipp M.,"The Economics of ICT Networks. Contribution to Economics Series. Physica-Verlag, Heidelberg, Germany,(2006)

5. Doganoglu, T. and Wright, J. : Multihoming and compatibility , Elsevier International Journal of Industrial Organization, vol.24, pp.45-67, (2005)
6. Schiff, A.:Open and closed systems of two-sided networks, Information Economics and Policy, pp.425-442,(2003)
7. Rochet, J.C. and Tirole, J.: Defining Two-Sided Markets, mimeo, Rochet: IDEI and GREMAQ, University of Toulouse and Tirole: IDEI and GREMAQ, University of Toulouse, CERAS, University of Paris, and MIT,(2004)
8. Rochet, J.C. and Tirole. J.: Two-Sided Markets: An Overview, mimeo, IDEI University of Toulouse. A preliminary version was presented at "The Economics of Two-Sided Markets" conference, held at the University of Toulouse, January, (2004)
9. Roson, R:Two-sided markets: a tentative survey, Review of Network Economics, vol 4, No. 2, pp.142–160, (2005)
10. Evans, D.S.: Some Empirical Aspects of Multi-Sided Platform Industries, Review of Network Economics, vol.2, pp. 191-209,(2003)
11. Wright, J.: Optimal card payment systems, Elsevier, European Economic Review, vol. 47, pp. 587-612 ,(2002)
12. Wright, J.: Pricing in debit and credit card schemes, Elsevier, Economics Letters, vol. 80, pp. 305-309, (2003)
13. Caillaud, B. and Jullien, B.: Chicken & Egg: Competition among Intermediation Service Providers, RAND Journal of Economics, vol. 34, pp.309-328, (2003)
14. Farrell, J.:Efficienty and Competition between Payment Instruments,Review of Network Economics, vol.5, pp.26-44,(2006)
15. Gabszewicz, J.J and Wauthy, X.Y: Two-Sided Markets and Price Competition with Multi-homing, Working Paper, (2004)
16. Guthrie, G. and Wright, J. :Competing Payment Schemes, Working Paper, (2006)
17. Manenti, F. and Somma, E:Plastic Clashes: Competition among Closed and Open Systems in the Credit Card Industry, Working Paper, (2003)
18. Rochet, J.C. and Tirole, J.:Cooperation among Competitors: Some Economics of Payment Card Associations, Rand Journal of Economics, vol. 33, pp. 549-570, (2002)
19. Rochet, J.C. and Tirole, J.: Platform Competition in Two-Sided Markets, Journal of European Economic Association, vol.1, pp. 990-1029, (2003).
20. Distaso, W., Lupi, P. and Manenti, F.M.: Platform competition and broadband uptake:Theory and empirical evidence from the European Union, Elsevier,Information Economics and Policy, vol. 18, pp. 87-106,(2006)
21. Milne, A. :What is in it for us? Network effects and bank payment innovation, Elsevier, Journal of Banking & Finance, vol. 30, pp. 1613-1630, (2005).
22. Zou,B: Vintage technology, optimal investment and technology adoption, Elsevier, Economic Modelling, vol.23,pp. 515-533 ,(2006)
23. Calabrese. A., Gastaldi. M., Iacovelli. I., Levialdi Ghiron. N: Innovation and competition in the two- sided markets: the case of the payment system, International Journal of Management and Network Economics, vol. 1, pp. 1-20, (2008)
24. Baumol W.J.: The Free-Market Innovation Machine: Analyzing the Growth Miracle of Capitalism, Princeton University Press, (2002)

OOPUS WEB: A MPC Customizing Platform with Ergonomic Planning Interfaces

Benjamin Klöpper[1], Tobias Rust[1], Thorsten Timm[1], Daniel Brüggemann, Wilhelm Dangelmaier[1],

[1] Heinz Nixdorf Institute, University of Paderborn,
33102 Paderborn, Germany
{kloepper, tobias.rust, ttimm, dbruegg, whd}@hni.upb.de

Abstract. Manufacturing planning and control (MPC) is a challenging task for decision support and planning systems. On the one hand side, the decision problems in this area are usually quite complex and have to be solved under severe time restrictions. On the other hand, MPC includes many soft restrictions and objectives, which can hardly be modeled in an information system. Thus, ergonomic support for human planners, which adapt and improve automatically generated plans, is essential. Furthermore, workshops, factories and products differ largely in their properties and the resulting requirements regarding decision support software. In this paper we introduce a customizing platform for MPC tools which offers ergonomic planning interfaces for human planners and dispatchers.

Keywords: MPC, Planning Table, Customizing, Visualization

1 Introduction

Manufacturing Planning and Control (MPC) is a critical task in many industries and it encompasses a large variety of decision problems [1]. This variety ranges from the design of production systems to the determination of production quantities and the sequencing of production lots on a machine. For these problems, a large number of formulations (e.g. as linear program) are available. For instance, Brucker [2] defines 66 different classes of basic scheduling problem. Pochet and Wolsey [3] define 72 classes of single item lotsizing problems. Specific technical or organizational properties of production problems largely increases the number of relevant problem formulations. Furthermore, MPC possesses features which differ from other application areas of decision support and optimization.

The first essential feature of MPC is the high frequency of decision-making. Decisions about production quantities and the matching of quantities to the available production capacities are made, or at least revised, several times a week or sometimes even several times a day. The reason for this high frequency is the changing environment: incoming orders, unexpected scrap rates or machine breakdowns.

The second feature is the lack of clearly defined objectives. From the view point of cost-effectiveness the overall purpose of MPC is to achieve a predetermined output performance at minimal costs [4]. Unfortunately, the exact determination of costs in a production environment is often not possible, because the costs either are not continuously documented or cannot be documented (e.g. the long-term costs of delayed delivers are hard to estimate). Thus, usually alternative objectives and constraints are used in MPC. As the alternative objectives bear conflicts, it is not possible to describe a common objective function for MPC problems [5]. On the other hand, experienced human planners are able to describe a decision making process, which leads to a good or at least acceptable result. Human planners are also able to modify existing plans in such a way, that they comply with soft factors, which can hardly be included in an automated decision making process (e.g. in-plant work time agreements). For this purpose, MPC tools must provide interactive interfaces [6].

Finally, every production system and process has some unique properties. These properties may result from organizational or technical issues. Anyway, these individual properties have to be included in order to achieve feasible or even high quality decisions. This opinion is supported by the fact that materials management and production planning are among the most frequently customized modules of ERP systems. Olhager and Selldin [7] present a survey about Swedish manufacturing firms, where 60.7% of the material management and 69.2% of the production planning modules were modified during the implementation.

The following design assumptions are concluded from the features described above:

- Since fast decision making is required, MPC tools should apply heuristics
- These heuristics have to be selected with respect to individual properties
- Thus, the data model must include the individual properties of the production system
- The system must enable human planners to analyze and alter automatically generated production plans

For these reasons, a custom-made MPC solution for every production system (plant or workshop) is required while there is also a need for intuitive graphical user interfaces and effective planning procedures. Thus, a desirable platform enables the required individuality and cost-effective development process at the same time. In this paper we will briefly introduce the customizing concept of the MPC development platform OOPUS WEB and focus on the graphical planning interfaces provided within this platform.

2 State of the Art

This section will give a brief overview about the state of the art in the relevant fields of manufacturing planning and control, the visualization of planning data and software reuse.

2.1 From MRP to APS-Systems

The well-known root of manufacturing planning and control systems is the material requirements planning. MRP systems translate an externally provided Master Schedule into time phased net requirements for sub-assemblies, components and raw materials [8]. Classical MRP provides material requirements in ignorance of finite capacities. Thus, the next step in the development was manufacturing resource planning (MRPII) [9]. The shortcomings of MRPII in managing production facilities orders, production plans, inventories, and especially the need to integrate these functions led to a new class of information systems called enterprise resource planning systems (ERP). The main advantage of ERP system is their integration of (almost) all business processes in an organization and IT in a single solution. Thus, ERP systems feature a rather monolithic architecture. This monolithic and complex architecture and the attempt to build applications that satisfy the needs and requirements of many industrial sectors are the reason for the high amount of consulting and training during an ERP rollout. Consulting (30.1%), training (13.8%) and an implementation team (12.0%) are the main cost drivers [7] of ERP implementations. Software products of smaller complexity and with more comprehensible functions and data models, tuned for current company or production site, may reduce these costs significantly.

Although the roots of ERP systems are MRP and MRPII, the manufacturing control capabilities of these systems are rather poor. While Material Requirements Planning is a core functionality of ERP systems, their capacity requirements planning (CRP) modules do not provide satisfactory solutions (for a detailed discussion of these drawbacks cf. [10]). Thus, Advanced Planning Systems are the next attempt to solve the problem of manufacturing planning and control. These systems have stronger planning and optimization capabilities then ERP systems. But still standard software like SAP APO [11] may not support the individual needs of a given production site. Thus, several general architectures and procedure models for the implementations of MPC solutions were made (cf. [12] and [6]). However, these approaches are mere guidelines for the development of individual software solutions. They do not provide a framework for intense reuse of software in the context of MPC tools.

Brehm et al. [13] suggest more flexible ERP solutions with the application of Federated ERP systems on the basis of Web Services and P2P networks. The basic idea is to choose the current best Web Service for a given business task. This approach has several shortcomings. It relies on a centrally defined database model, which has to be accepted by all Web Services and ERP systems [14]. This severe prerequisite complicates the inclusion of workshop specific properties in the planning process. Furthermore, the XML based interaction between Web Services is not adequate for mass data usually processed in MPC systems.

2.2 Visualization und User Interfaces in MPC

The complexity and the dynamic of MPC clearly require ergonomic user interfaces and meaningful and expressive visualization of planning information to support the decision of a human planner [15]. Though, standard software for MPC does not provide such user interfaces [16]. For instance, SAP APO provides on the level of detailed production planning only a merely textual planning table without graphical visualization of the current demand fulfillment, the current capacity situation or a visualization of the currently implemented production schedule [17].

Research on the visualization of production planning data is mainly done for individual use cases ([16], [17]). A customizing platform for MPC in serial production obviously has to feature visualization concepts and interactive user interfaces which are applicable to many production scenarios and are flexible regarding details about the data to visualize.

3 The OOPUS WEB Approach

OOPUS WEB is a platform to fast and efficiently create individualized planning and scheduling tools. It provides flexible and adaptable master data functions as well as smart planning interfaces, which enable maximal information transparency for dispatchers. MPC Toolbox is intended to provide components and tools for a MPC tool product line.

The basic principle of OOPUS WEB is to decouple MPC algorithms and user interfaces from the data model of the platform. In this way, the large variety of planning algorithms and models is available and may be selected depending on the current application scenario. OOPUS WEB focuses on the area of serial production in line production fashion. This limitation enables the definition of a lean but extensible data model. This data model is the basis of the OOPUS WEB platform. The Model of Serial Manufacturing is described in detail in [15].

3.1 OOPUS WEB Technical Architecture

OOPUS WEB is entirely implemented in Java and all used packages and frameworks are open source. This enables an unproblematic distribution of the software for research and teaching. In the technical implementation, the focus is on flexibility as well. A thin client architecture (realized by a web browser interface) limits necessary maintenance. The entire business logic is executed on a servlet container; the users' workstations are limited to the user interfaces. The open source frameworks Hibernate and Tapestry assure the required decoupling between the presentation logic, business logic and the persistent data storage. Tapestry enables the implementation of web-applications according to the Model-View-Controller paradigm, thus user interfaces can be efficiently adapted to changing requirements [16]. Hibernate [17] decouples the business and presentation logic from the currently used database scheme and automatically creates a JavaBean representation of database schemes. Planning interfaces, which feature a more intense interaction with the user, are realized as Java applets. Again, all business logic and data management is kept on the server. Servlets, which interact with the applets, encapsulate the business logic and data access.

To embed OOPUS WEB into existing IT infrastructures, it is necessary to interact with classical ERP software. This concerns standing data (e.g. products and resources) as well as dynamic data (stocks, primary demands, and production schedules). The exchange of data is bidirectional. Up to now, OOPUS WEB implements an interface to the ERP system SAP ECC on basis of the JavaConnector.

3.2 OOPUS WEB Task Model

Fig. 1 shows the task structure of OOPUS WEB. The task structure is the fundamental architectural concept in OOPUS WEB. The overall task, the detailed planning and scheduling of a given production process is decomposed in several subtasks, each working on a section of the overall model. Such a section or sub model consists in partial subsets of production stages (multiple stage planning methods), a single production stage (single stage planning methods) or even a single line (single machine planning methods). Furthermore, the overall model is also divided into sub models regarding the granularity of planning periods. In that way, it is possible to perform a planning and scheduling on the level of months, weeks, days or shifts or to directly create a machine scheduling down to the minute. To solve a subtask, modules are combined and applied, which can be selected from a toolbox.

These modules are defined task oriented. Thus, a module is either a user interface, which enables the user to trigger algorithms or manipulate data regarding a certain task. Two different types of modules and components are distinguished in OOPUS WEB: user interfaces and algorithms.

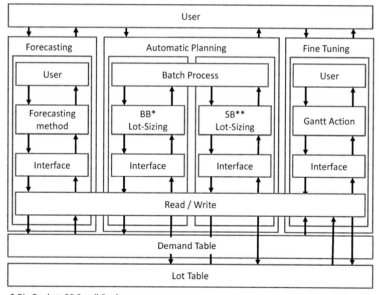

* Big Bucket ** Small Bucket

Fig. 1: Task structure of a use case for OOPUS WEB

95

3.3 Flexible Module Integration

To enable the maximum flexibility of OOPUS WEB the modules are not hard coded to the underlying database scheme. Instead, every module uses an internal data representation and provides a number of getter- and setter-methods to read and manipulate the internal model. Interface classes provide the access to the database. They perform a translation from the database scheme into the internal representation of the model. Thus, the modules can interact with various database schemes. Nevertheless, for every new database scheme, new interfaces classes have to be implemented. To limit this additional implementation effort, a code generator for interface classes was developed. A XML file defines the mapping between the current database scheme and a module's internal model. Several blocks describe the derivation of input parameters from the possible JavaBeans (which Hibernate automatically derives from the database) or the re-calculation of output variables. Such a block contains two types of elements. The first type of elements are parametrizable Hibernate queries, which specify the required data from the database. Calculation instructions are the second type. They calculate the values of the input parameters from the JavaBeans. XSLT code generation [18] is used to create an individual interface class. The automated interface generation supports two different types of interfaces. The first kind of interface treats the methods and algorithms as a black box. It derives all required data, calls the algorithm, receives the results of the calculation, and writes them into the database. This kind of interface is suitable for many planning and optimization algorithms and requires no modification or specific programming within the implementation of the algorithm. This is an important property, if existing implementations shall be reused. The left part of Fig. 2 illustrates the processing scheme of the black box interface.

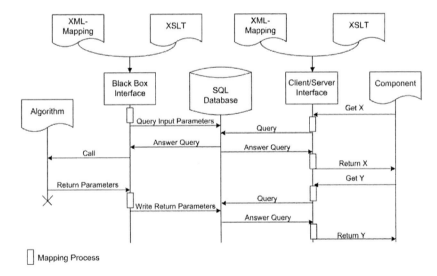

Fig. 2: Interaction Scheme for Automatically Generated Interfaces

96

On the other hand, this kind of interface implies that all required data is known in advance. This condition cannot be held true for every algorithm and especially not for every component of the platform. Especially when user interaction is involved (like in manual planning), it is not possible to comply with this precondition. Thus, the second kind of interface allows a more client/server-like interaction between the methods or components and the database. Of course, these interfaces require a OOPUS WEB specific programming style. The methods or user interfaces must be able to call get/set methods provided by the interface.

4 OOPUS WEB Planning Interfaces

A MPC configuration platform requires interactive planning interfaces for different application scenarios. To avoid manual implementation efforts, the interactive planning interfaces should be reusable. A task that requires strong visualization support is the solution and manual adaption of lot-sizing and sequencing problems. Thus, we decided to design interactive planning interfaces for the two fundamental types of lot-sizing problems: small bucket and big bucket lot-sizing problems.

In small bucket problems, usually one product (and at maximum up to two products) can be produced in a time period. Thus, small bucket problems contain information about the sequence of products in the production process. This information enables the consideration of sequence dependent set-up times. If sequence dependent set-up times are relevant to the production process (the variance of set-up times is quite large), this type of model is suitable.

In big bucket problems, more than one product can be produced in time period. These models contain no information about the sequence which is used to produce the material in the specific time period. Thus, no sequence dependent information about setup times can be included. Big bucket problems usually result in smaller optimization problems and are thus easier to solve. They are applicable if sequence dependent set-up times are not important or can be used to generate an approximate master plan, which is used to define a number of small bucket problems (one for each big bucket time period).

4.1 Small Bucket Planning

One main issue of OOPUS WEB is to present the large number of planning relevant data in a highly ergonomic way. The main approach to realize this for an up-to-the-minute-planning is the idea of two functional split but data coupled graphical user interfaces. The planning table displays the lots on their assembly lines over time in form of a Gantt chart. Gantt charts are a popular method to visualize the result of scheduling or small bucket planning processes [19]. The planner can directly change the plan by different lot actions like moving or changing the lot size.

The plan visualized in the planning table is shown in a cumulative quantity table by its forecasted cumulative quantities where it can be compared with the demands. The cumulative quantity concept [20] is a representation used in serial production to clearly show changes of dates and quantities.

The OOPUS WEB small bucket planning table (Fig. 3) enables up to the minute-planning.

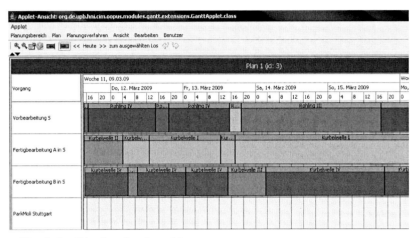

Fig. 3: Small bucket planning table

At the very top of the planning table is the action and navigation area where the user can execute fundamental planning actions and change the appearance of the Gantt chart. There are several zoom levels, thus the user can adapt the view to his needs. The zoom levels enable the user to look at the plan in a very detailed level as well as to get a good overview of the capacity utilization in a bigger time period.

Below is the main area of the planning table where all lots are visualized on the assembly lines and where the plan can directly be changed by different actions on the lots. The yellow line indicates a line where lots can be intermediately placed for re-planning.

The user can manipulate the plan in three different ways:

1) automatic planning
2) semi-automatic planning
3) manual planning

1) Automatic planning

To create a completely new plan, based on the customer requests and the planned capacities, the user can start an automatic planning algorithm or a combination of planning algorithms. The algorithms can be chosen from the MPC-Toolbox.

2) Semi-automatic planning

The small bucket planning table also offers semi-automatic functions to change the current plan. Some of these are:

- Fix the lots that should persist and plan the rest automatically

- Create a lot based on an open demand
- Move a lot to an open demand
- Change the lot size based on an open demand

3) Manual planning

OOPUS WEB offers a very easy and intuitive moving of lots via drag & drop. After a move the lot production time is recalculated dynamically. The production time may be change due to capacities of shifts and included breaks. In this case, the size of the lot on the Gantt chart is changed as well. OOPUS WEB ensures that lots can only be moved to assembly lines where they are allowed to produce and that they do not start or end in areas which are not productive like breaks or weekends. OOPUS WEB guarantees that there are no overlaying lots. The behavior which is executed when a user moves a lot over another lot can be configured by the planner via so called *bulldozer* functionality. If this functionality is disabled two lots are planned in a row without a gap between them and all lots except the moved lot will keep their position. If the function is enabled the position of the moved lot will be fixed and the other lots are moved to either the history or the future which can be configured as well.

The same plan is updated in the corresponding cumulative quantity table (CQT) when the plan was changed. The CQT (Fig. 4) gives an overview of the manufacturing program which has to be realized and of the manufacturing program which would be realized by exact adherence of the actual viewed plan. Thereby the planner is able to detect mismatches of planned and required product quantities easily. Exactly these mismatches have to be avoided, because they can lead to high costs. In addition to this information, several other parameters like free capacities of assembly lines or lot parameters are shown to support the planner in creating a plan which can satisfy the fixed dates for all orders.

Vorgang	Verbrauchsfaktor	SollFSZ	IstFSZ	Diff.		Fr 13.03.09	Sa 14.03.09	So 15.03.09
Fertigbearbeitung A in S					AT	Ja	Nein	Nein
					Schichten	3	0	0
					Kapazität	1380	120	0
	Kurbelwelle I	2087			Soll-FSZ	2087	2087	2087
			327		Plan-FSZ	327	327	366
				-1760	Differenz	-1760	-1760	-1721
					Soll-diskret	0	0	0
					Plan-Vorgang	0	0	39
	Kurbelwelle II	2058			Soll-FSZ	2058	2058	2058
			447		Plan-FSZ	478	478	478
				-1611	Differenz	-1580	-1580	-1580
					Soll-diskret	0	0	0
					Plan-Vorgang	31	0	0
	Kurbelwelle III	2536			Soll-FSZ	2536	2536	2536
			520		Plan-FSZ	552	552	598
				-2016	Differenz	-1984	-1984	-1938

Fig. 4: Cumulative quantity table

The described small bucket planning can be configured to the requirements of the planner, e.g. by considering sequence dependent setup times, by choosing different time granularities or by enabling different functionalities for semi-automatic planning.

4.2 Big Bucket Planning

For big bucket planning a different visualization concept with a single graphical user interface was developed for OOPUS WEB, the big bucket planning table (Fig. 5).

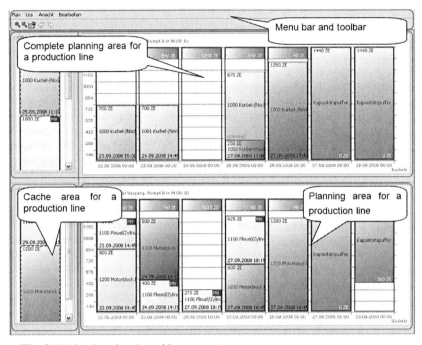

Fig. 5: Big bucket planning table

The menu bar at the top offers important functions, like changes of planning parameters or zooming. Below the menu bar is a planning area for each considered production line. This area is split into two parts. On the left side open demands are visualized in a so called cache. On the right side is the production area where lots are assigned to buckets on production lines.

The planner can use the cache to detect open demands which needs to be assigned to a bucket. He can plan open demands as lots by moving them into the planning area on the right side. Open demands are ordered by their due dates though the planner can plan the earliest demands first.

The right part of the planning table shows the plan with its lots in their assigned buckets. The size of a bucket can be chosen by the planner, Fig. 4 shows buckets with the duration of one day. On top of each bucket a grey block shows capacity information for the bucket. It blocks the space where lots can be placed by displaying the difference to the maximal capacity and gives information about the available time in a bucket. The capacity depends on the planned shift model which is used in the bucket. There is a functionality to adjust the capacity and hence alter the shift model directly from the planning table.

The lots also give important information to the planner. On top they show the capacity which is required on the planned production line. In the middle the identifier for the part number is shown. Important is the due date on the lower right of the lot. Depending on the planned date of a lot compared to its due date the way of displaying the date changes. It is shown in red when a lot is planned with delay. If a surplus is planned the planner can see this by the missing of the due date. The upper right part of a lot shows if a lot can be produced on different production lines. This makes it easier for the planner to search for free spaces if he wants to move the lot.

There are some other features which support the planner in creating a good plan. For example the colors of the time buckets are changed if the planner starts dragging a lot. Every bucket which time slot is before the due date and which is assigned to a valid production line is displayed in green. Every bucket that would lead to a delay or which is part of an invalid production line is shown in red. By this visualization the planner can directly see the consequence of his action. It is possible to plan a lot with a delay, but it is not possible to plan it on a line where the product is not assigned to.

These two configurable visualization concepts are suitable for many different planning scenarios. They don't have to be used independently, but can also be combined though that first a big bucket planning is executed which is the basis for the following small bucket planning.

5 Conclusion and further work

In this paper we introduced the special challenges of decision support in manufacturing planning and control (MPC) and derived the conclusion, that there is need for support in the development of individual solutions, which consider the individual properties of workshops and factories. The platform OOPUS WEB enables an efficient development of such individual solutions. It enables extensive reuse of existing software and applies a configuration approach to support the individual requirements.

Since the support of human planner with ergonomic user interfaces is a critical issue in MPC application, we introduced two types of planning interfaces provided by OOPUS WEB. The small bucket and big bucket planning tables support the two fundamental types of production planning and scheduling problems and are thus suitable for a generalized approach like OOPUS WEB.

Further work can be done regarding the support of new planning functionalities, such as forecasting or shift and capacity planning.

References

1. Tempelmeier, H., Kuhn, H.: Flexible Manufacturing Systems: Decision Support for Design and Operation. Wiley-Interscience, San Francisco (1993)
2. Brucker, P.: Scheduling Algorithms, Springer Verlag, Berlin (2007)

3. Pochet, Y. and Wolsey, L.: Production Planning by Mixed Integer Programming. Springer Verlag, Berlin (2007)
4. Vollmann, T.E., Berry, W.L., Whybark, D.C., Jacobs, F.R.: Manufacturing Planning and Control for Supply Chain Management, McGraw-Hill, Boston (2005)
5. Fleischmann, B., Meyr, H., Wagner, M.: Advanced Planning. In: Stadtler, H., Kilger, C.: Supply Chain Management and Advanced Planning, Springer Verlag, Berlin
6. Stadtler, H.: Production Planning and Scheduling. In: Stadtler, H., Kilger, C.: Supply Chain Management and Advanced Planning, Springer Verlag, Berlin (2005)
7. Olhager, J., Selldin, E.: Enterprise resource planning survey of Swedish manufacturing firms. European Journal of Operational Research 146, 365—373 (2003)
8. Plossl, G.: Orlicky's Material Requirements Planning, 2nd edition, McGrawHill, New York (1994)
9. Higgins, P., LeRoy, P., Tierney, L.: Manufacturing Planning and Control: Beyond MRP II. Springer Verlag, Berlin (1996)
10. Tempelmeier, H., Derstroff, M.: A lagranean heuristic for mulit-item mulit-level constrained lotsizing with setup times. Management Science, 42, pp. 738-757 (1996)
11. Balla, J.: Production Planing with SAP APO-PP/DS, Galileo SAP PRESS (2006)
12. Zijm, W.H.M.:. Towards intelligent manufacturing planning and control systems. OR Spektrum, 22, pp. 313-345 (2000)
13. Brehm, N., Marx Gomez, J., Rautenstrauch, C.: An ERP Solution Based on Web Services and Peer-to-Peer networks, in: International Journal of Information Technology and Management, Bd. 1 (2007).
14. Brehm, N., Marx Gomez, J.: Web Service-Based Specification and Implementation of Functional Components in Federated ERP-Systems, in: Abramowicz, W. (Hrsg.), Business Information Systems 2007, LNCS, Bd. 4439, Berlin, 133-146.
15. Dangelmaier, W., Timm, T., Klöpper, B., Brüggemann, D.: A Modelling Approach for Dynamic and Complex Capacities in Production Control Systems. In: Abramowic, W. : Business Information Systems, LNCS, 4439, 626 – 637, Springer, Heidelberg (2007)
16. Ship, H.M.L.: Tapestry in Action, Manning, Greenwich (2004)
17. Bauer, C., King, G.: Java Persistance with Hibernate. Manning, Greenwich (2004)
18. Cleaveland, J.C.: Program Generators with SM and Java. Prentice Hall, Upper Saddle River (2001)
19. Wilson, J.M.: Gantt Charts: A centenary appreciation. European Journal of Operations Research, 149, pp. 430-437 (2003)
20. Schönsleben, P.: Integrales Logistikmanagement - Planung und Steuerung der umfassenden Supply Chain. Springer Verlag, Berlin, 4th edition (2004)

Empirical Research on Technology-Related Privacy Concerns

Cliona McParland, Regina Conolly
Dublin City University,
Dublin 9, Ireland
{ cliona.mcparland2@mail.dcu.ie, Regina.connolly@dcu.ie}

Abstract: The exponential adoption of the Internet for transaction and interaction purposes continues unabated. However, despite the obvious empowering benefits of the Internet, consumers concerns regarding the ability of online vendors to collect and use information regarding them and their online interactions have also increased. Vendors facing intense competition in the marketplace are under increasing pressure to gain a more sophisticated understanding of their consumers and thus view the collection of consumers' personal and interaction information as essential to achieving that understanding. Awareness of this fact has accentuated consumers' privacy concerns and in some cases impacted interaction intentions and behaviour. Similarly, in the computer-mediated work environment, employees' awareness that communication-monitoring technologies are being used to monitor their email and Internet interactions has increased. Despite the importance of this issue, research on technology-related privacy concerns remains in an embryonic stage. Moreover, the literature indicates that much confusion surrounds the construct and in many studies the construct is neither clearly defined nor operationalised. The aim of this paper is therefore to reduce that confusion by providing a brief review of the literature while outlining potential research avenues worthy of future research. This paper provides researchers with a refined and holistic understanding of the construct and consequently makes a valuable contribution not only to information systems research but also to practitioners in their efforts to better understand the factors that predict and inhibit technology-related privacy concerns.

Keywords: Privacy, Consumer information, Consumer behavior, Frameworks, Empirical research.

1 Introduction

Privacy has long been a contentious issue as individuals strive to protect their personal information from misuse by others. In the social science literature the importance of individuals' privacy concerns is widely acknowledged (e.g Konvitz, 1966; Powers, 1996; Froomkin, 2000; Rule, 2004; Cassidy and Chae, 2006) and it is recognised as a dynamic issue that has the potential to impact attitudes, perceptions, and even the environment and future technology developments (Crompton, 2001).

From an information systems perspective however, empirical research on technology-related privacy concerns still remains at an embryonic stage and furthermore the limited number of studies on the construct that do exist tend to be limited in size and nature (Gefen and Straub, 2000; Cockcroft and Heales, 2005). Compounding the problem is the fact that some of these studies are beset by conflicting conceptualisations of the construct, as well as a lack of agreement regarding the factors that predict the perceptions, attitudes and behaviours of the individuals themselves. Consequently, it is difficult for privacy researchers within the information systems field to compare and contrast the results of previous studies in their efforts to progress understanding of the construct.

Although the literature on technology-related privacy is limited, what does exist tends to focus on the online marketplace and the fact that consumers are becoming increasingly aware of the ways in which online vendors can collect and use potentially sensitive information regarding them and their actions without their express permission. From a vendor perspective their ability to collate such data allows them to provide customers with specifically customised information thus offering them a personalised shopping experience. From a consumer perspective however, the price of this personalised shopping experience may outweigh any customisation benefits, particularly when vendors have been known to sell information on consumers to third parties without their knowledge or consent. Within the information systems discipline however, technology-related privacy concerns are stretching further afield so that there is now an increasing awareness of the importance of technology-related privacy concerns within the computer-mediated work environment also. Most individuals are accustomed to a certain degree of privacy in their daily lives however the increasing proliferation of technologies into our working environments has resulted in numerous situations whereby the right to invade the privacy of the employee is being taken for granted by management (Nord et al., 2006).

The aim of this study therefore is to provide both a concise and consolidated review of the technology-related privacy literature. While this paper focuses heavily on privacy concerns from within both the electronic marketplace and the computer-mediated work environment, focus will also be drawn towards the conceptual confusion surrounding the privacy construct itself and the need for clarity in the literature.

2. The Privacy Construct

Privacy is a complex construct that has received the attention of researchers from a broad spectrum of disciplines including ethics (Platt, 1995), economics (Rust et al., 2002), marketing (Graeff and Harmon, 2002), management (Robey, 1979) as well as from the legal discipline even as far back as 1860 (Warren and Brandeis). However, despite this interest, the construct remains beset by conceptual and operational confusion. For example, Tavani (1999) remarks that privacy is neither clearly understood nor clearly defined while Introna (1996) comments that for every definition of privacy, it is also possible to find a counterexample in the literature. As a result, many researchers choose to define privacy specific to the focus of their specific study or the lens of their discipline in an attempt to evade this problem (Smith, 2001) and as a consequence the conceptual confusion that surrounds the construct remains undiminished. Unsurprisingly, these differing conceptualisations have manifested in similarly differing views regarding how the construct should be examined and measured. For example, privacy researchers within the legal discipline argue that privacy should be measured in terms of the rights of the individual whilst ethics researchers contend that the morality of privacy protection mechanisms for the individual should be the focus of research attention. Interestingly, and perhaps most sensibly, some economics researchers (Parker 1974, Acquisti, 2002, Rust *et al.*, 2002) argue that in order to gain a full understanding of the privacy construct it is necessary to examine it from a multiplicity of viewpoints. Consequently, Parker (1974) maintains that privacy can be examined as a psychological state, a form of power, an inherent right or an aspect of freedom. More recently, Acquisti (2004) has emphasised the multi-dimensional nature of the construct and posited that privacy should no longer be viewed as a single unambiguous concept, but become a class of multifaceted interests.

One aspect of privacy on which many researchers concur is the central to its understanding is the issue of control, specifically the individual's need to have control over their personal information. Practitioner reports also confirm the importance that consumers attribute to being able to control their personal information (e.g Harris, 2004) Control is defined as *"the power of directing command, the power of restraining"* (Oxford, 1996: 291) and is consistently proposed in the literature as a key factor in relation to understanding consumer privacy concerns. For example, Westin (1967) argues that privacy is the claim of individuals, groups, or institutions to decipher for themselves when, how and to what extent their personal information is conveyed to others. This issue of personal control is widely supported by researchers such as Fried (1968: 482) who defines privacy as the *"control we have over information about ourselves"* and Parker (1974: 281) who defines privacy in terms of the *"control over who can sense us"*. Personal control is important as it relates to the interest of individuals to control or significantly influence the handling of personal data (Clarke, 1988).

However, a diverse body of researchers dispute the relevance of control in understanding privacy concerns. They argue that to define privacy in terms of control can yield a narrow perspective as not every loss or gain of control over information constitutes a loss or gain of privacy (Parker, 1974). For example, all online consumers who voluntarily provide personal information in the course of their transactions do not necessarily view that as a loss of control and consequently a loss of privacy. Even the knowledge that each of their online interactions is providing the vendor with a potential trail of information regarding who they are, their buying habits and other personal details does not necessarily constitute a lack of control or a loss or privacy in the eyes of such consumers. With that in mind, some researchers (Moor 1990, 1997; Schoeman 1984) suggest that it would be better to focus on the issue of restricted access rather than on consumer's need for control when trying to understand technology-related privacy issues.

While agreement as to the relevance of control in relation to understanding privacy remains a disputed issue, the attention placed on this issue by researchers' points to the fact that privacy comprises ethical or moral dimensions. Ethics is the branch of philosophy that deals with theories of right and wrong behaviour and privacy issues have frequently been discussed in this in relation to ethical impacts. For example, the increasing pervasiveness of technologies into human beings' work and leisure environments has opened up a spectrum of unregulated behaviour and previously accepted distinctions regarding correct and immoral behaviour are no longer always clear (Turban, 2006). For example, ethical questions surround the issue of surveillance – and in particular electronic surveillance - which according to Clarke (1988) is the systematic monitoring of the actions or communication of individuals. Within computer-mediated work environments, the critical need to protect the employee's privacy rights is becoming increasingly apparent as modern technologies provide the opportunity for continuous data collection. In some cases individuals may be conscious that they are being monitored, they are just not sure of the extent and detail of that monitoring. Neither are they aware of how that collated information is being employed by the monitoring body. Researchers such as Safire (2002) note how extreme pervasive surveillance tends to result in a 'creepy feeling' among those being monitored despite the fact that they have done nothing wrong to merit such scrutiny. In fact, the monitoring of employees' computer-related interactions has previously been described as an 'electronic whip' used unfairly by management (Tavani, 2004).

In summary, privacy has been defined in the literature from a multiplicity of viewpoints, which has resulted in definitional and operational confusion regarding the construct. As we enter the third millennium we have turned the corner into a place where technology pervades our day-to-day lives, and many things which would previously have been considered flights of imagination, are as a result of technology, becoming part of our reality (Kostakos *et al.*, 2005, Galanxhi and Fui-Hoon 2004). Consequently, the need for an improved understanding of the nature of technology-related privacy construct has increased rather than diminished.

2.2 Privacy, Trust and Uncertainty in an Online Environment

While consumer privacy has always been a significant issue in the traditional offline market, it has assumed a greater importance with the increased adoption of the Internet (Rust *et al.*, 2002). The nature of the electronic environment has brought issues of trust, risk and uncertainty centre stage. For example the literature recognises the importance of trust in the specific business-to-consumer on-line transaction domain (Lee and Turban, 2001; Gefen and Straub, 2000; Reichheld and Schefter, 2000). In fact Ratnasingham (1998) contends that the influence of trust on interactions is even more crucial in the pervasive online environment than in the physical and traditional marketplace. Similarly, the Cheskin eCommerce Trust Study (1999: 2) notes that as *"the Internet develops and matures, its success will depend in large part on gaining and maintaining the trust of visitors. This will be paramount to sites that depend on consumer commerce."* However, despite the fact that trust is a rare commodity which is built up slowly over time (Tracy, 1995) and building and maintaining it is essential for the survival of any relationship, it is a fragile bond that can be destroyed easily. In order for trust to be engendered therefore, consumers must be confident that their personal information will not be used without their consent and will not be sold to third parties. Those companies that are successful at building that trust and managing the uncertainty associated with consumer disclosure of personal information will benefit from increased consumer confidence.

The individual's need to trust relates directly to the risk involved in a given situation (Mayer *et al.,* 1995). In the business-to-consumer electronic commerce environment the degree of risk is even greater than in the traditional commercial environment (Grabner-Krauter and Kaluscha, 2003) therefore the need for trust is correspondingly greater. For example, purchasing on the Internet holds risks that are unique to that context. These include the requirement to provide sensitive information, and the uncertainty of what the retailer will do with the consumer's personal information (Grabner-Krauter and Kaluscha, 2003). In fact, it has been shown that awareness of their lack of control over personal data can lead to consumers withholding information from companies and resisting the adoption of online purchasing (Goldsmith and Bridges, 2000). Due to this lack of control and uncertainty, many consumers simply do not trust most web providers enough to engage in relationship exchanges with them (Hoffman *et al.,* 1999).

Hirschleifer and Riley's (1979) theory of information can also be used to better understand the uncertainty that applies to the on-line purchase environment. This theory outlines two categories of uncertainty: *system-dependent uncertainty* and *transaction-specific uncertainty*. Both types of uncertainty exist in the online purchase environment. For example, the online consumer is dependent on the technological medium for the process to take place effectively and securely but not have any control over the medium or the transmission of the data (*system-dependent uncertainty*). *Transaction-specific uncertainty* includes the possibility that even when guarantees are provided that customer data will not be passed on to third parties, the consumer does not have any guarantee that the vendor has measures in place to protect consumer data from employee theft. Hence, there is a high level of uncertainty related to the on-line purchase environment. The uncertainty and lack of control related to the online environment reflects the significant asymmetry that exists in terms of what the Internet means to individuals versus vendors. For example, Prakhaber (2000) rightly points out that while the technology has created better, faster and cheaper ways for businesses to meet their customers' needs and better faster and cheaper ways for customers to satisfy their own needs, the capability to leverage this technology is far higher for companies than for individual consumers. Because unequal forces, leading to asymmetric information availability, tilt the playing field significantly in favour of industry, such technologies do not create market benefit to all parties in an equitable manner.

While marketers need information on consumers in order to refine products and services to increase consumer satisfaction, the need to find a way in which the interests of both consumers and marketers can be served has never been more urgent. Often the information that is collated on consumers is done so without their consent thus exacerbating privacy concerns. Moreover it is apparent that not all researchers acknowledge the extent of this problem. For example, Hoyer and MacInnis (1997) maintain that one of the main reasons why privacy concerns regarding online vendors' collection of consumer information exist is due to consumers' lack of understanding regarding how this information is collected and more importantly how it will benefit them. Other researchers, such as Ratnasingham (1998) dispute this notion, arguing that customers concerns and anxieties regarding transaction confidentiality and anonymity are frequent and legitimate and should therefore be acknowledged as such.

In this environment, businesses have a choice as to how they should respond thus determining the type of buyer-seller relationships that their company has. If privacy concerns are not addressed they manifest through the costs of lost sales, through the move from online to offline business channels and through lost customer relationships. The ownership of online consumers will be predicated to a large degree on the way in which businesses seeking to leverage Internet technology gather market information whilst equally embracing the responsibility of preserving consumer privacy.

3 Analysis of the Empirical Literature

In the literature, technology-related privacy concerns have mainly been considered from a transactional perspective, with the concerns of the online consumer paramount to the discussion. However, such concerns are equally salient and critical in the organisational employment context. Therefore, in this paper, in order to provide a thorough review of the literature, the studies of technology-related privacy issues have been grouped into two main categories – consumer concerns and employee concerns. Information regarding how the authors selected their samples and the methodology used is also provided.

While the privacy literature specific to consumers' technology-related privacy concerns is remarkably limited, a number of studies stand out as deserving of comment. Udo's (2001) study of 158 online users examined their attitudes in relation to privacy and security concerns. He found privacy ranked as the highest concern among users' with threats to security and to children coming in a close second and third. Interestingly, the study findings indicate that for every three shoppers in the study who were willing to purchase on-line, there are seven others who are too concerned to shop in the virtual marketplace. Based on an analysis of the results the author concluded that privacy and security threats are the main barriers to e-commerce success and therefore must be dealt with accordingly.

A more detailed study of the privacy concerns that attempted to classify individuals in terms of their level of privacy concern was conducted by Sheehan (2002). She employed Westin's (1967) tripartite grouping of Internet users (pragmatists, unconcerned, privacy fundamentalists) as a guide and categorised 889 online users in terms of the degree to which are concerned about engaging in on-line transactions. An online survey consisting of 15 privacy related statements representing 5 different factors that can influence privacy concerns were administered to the study participants who were then measured in terms of their level of response to three different privacy scenarios. The results showed that the majority of the respondents (81%) were pragmatists in relation to their privacy concerns, 16% of the respondents were classified as being unconcerned with the remaining 3% meeting the classification standard of privacy fundamentalists. While the author recognises the limited generality of Westin's typology, the study findings are interesting in that they point to the fact that online privacy concerns are likely to be contextually driven rather than the result of embedded psychological constructs specific to the individual.

Singh and Hill's (2003) study employed duty-based theories, social contract theory and stakeholder theories to examine the attitudes of 106 German consumers in relation to their online privacy concerns. A pencil and paper survey was administered to depict the attitudes of German consumers' towards privacy in general but more specially to Internet privacy. A 5 point likert scale measured the attitudinal responses of the respondents with only standard demographic data being considered in the results. Interestingly, the issue of control surfaced in this study with the findings identifying a strong desire among German consumers' to have some level of control over how their personal information is collated, disclosed or used. The study further highlighted the importance of online vendor responsibility and the active role the Government should play in protecting citizens' privacy. Although it is unlikely that this desire for control over personal information is limited to German consumers, whether or not this applies across other European countries remains undetermined due to dearth of cross-cultural research on this subject.

While Malthotra et al., (2004) developed a scale and casual model to determine the dimensionality of an Internet users' information privacy concerns (in terms of data collection, control and awareness), they note that development of this scale was highly dependent on contextual factors and does not examine the influence of privacy concerns on actual behaviour. While they suggest that opportunities for future research in this area are abundant, it is clear that the need for a reliable culture-independent measurement instrument to measure information privacy concerns has not yet been met.

Whilst most studies have focused on the attitudes of online consumers in relation to privacy, a recent study conducted by Van Slyke et al., (2006) extends previous models of e-commerce adoption to investigate the degree to which consumers' information privacy concerns influence behavioural outcome i.e. their willingness to partake in transactions on-line. Two privacy measurement instruments were applied in this study – one to measure privacy concerns in relation to a high recognition website and the second to privacy concerns in relation to a less well known website. The study's findings show that privacy concerns, perceived risk and familiarity with the website play a significant role in consumers' willingness to transact online. However, contrary to previous studies (such as Malthotra et al., 2004) a positive relationship between information privacy concerns and level of trust was identified in the study. Van Slyke et al., (2006) suggest the trade-off nature of the online relationship, where information is exchanged in return for a transaction to take place, may in part explain this abnormality of this finding. Again, the lack of research on this topic and in particular comparable studies with similar type sample in other countries makes it difficult to determine whether this outcome pertains only to the authors sample or is an indication of a more complex dynamic at work. In fact, all of the above mentioned studies, except that of Singh and Hill, were conducted in the United States, emphasising the lack of research on technology-related privacy concerns from a European perspective.

A number of studies do not examine privacy issues specifically but rather include it amongst a number of variables that are being measured (e.g. Flavian and Guinaliu, 2006; Chen and Barnes, 2007). For example, Joines et al.,'s (2003) study of the influence of demographics and motivational factors on Internet use includes a measure of privacy along with other measures, whilst Lancelot Miltgen's (2007) study focuses on the factors that influence online consumers' decisions to provide personal information as opposed to directly focusing on privacy concerns. Similarly, a number of technology adoption studies include a measure of privacy but do not focus on it uniquely (e.g. Pavlou and Fygenson, 2006; Shih, 2004). The same holds true for many studies that examine the antecedents of trust in electronic commerce (e.g. Cheung and Lee, 2001) where the influence of privacy concerns are examined along with other measures such as security in terms of their influence on behavioural outcome. Table 1 below provides a sample of the literature directly focusing on technology-related consumer concerns.

Table 1. Studies of Technology-Related Consumer Concerns

Study	Context	Sample	Methodology
Udo (2001)	Examine privacy and security concerns of online users'	158 participants USA	29 item online questionnaire
Sheehan (2002)	Examines online consumers to see if their concerns match those in an offline environment.	889 online respondents. USA	Online survey
Singh and Hill (2003)	Focus on consumer Internet concerns	106 online consumers. Germany	Paper and pencil survey.
Malhotra et al. (2004)	Developed internet users privacy concerns measurement instrument (IUIPC)	449 respondents USA	Instrument developed through scenario testing
Van Slyke *et al.,* (2006)	Assesses the degree to which consumers' information privacy concerns affect their willingness to engage in online transactions.	Two samples were used, one representing a well known merchant (713) the other representing a less well known merchant (287) USA	Survey

Whilst much attention has focused on internet users information privacy concerns, privacy concerns are equally important in the context of the computer-mediated work environment, particularly as most individuals spend significant amounts of their time in such contexts. For example, the use of email and Internet in the workplace has increased management fears relating to the loss of trade secrets through an aggrieved employee and the fear that offensive or explicit material could be used by an employeed resulting in adverse publicity for the company (Laudon and Laudon, 2001). Consequently, it is estimated that nearly 80% of all organisations now employ some level of employee surveillance (termed dataveillance) in the day to day running of the company (D'Urso, 2006). While organisations frequently have a number of legitimate reasons to monitor their employees' internet activities, researchers such as Kierkegaard (2005) emphasise the need to investigate the level of control an employer should have over an employees' electronic communications and the degree to which employees should be concerned about this surveillance of the workplace. Other researchers (Alder *et al.,* 2006) concur and emphasise that there are valid concerns regarding the impact of internet monitoring on employees attitudes and behaviours.

Despite a remarkably limited number of studies on this issue (Boehle, 2000), those few studies that do exist provide interesting insights into the importance of this issue and its potential for research. For example, Stanton and Weiss' (2000) study examined the issue of electronic monitoring from both the employer and employee perspective. A three part survey was derived from a longer semi-structured research instrument used by the authors in a previous study. A surveillance-related question deliberately worded with both positive and negative connotations acted as the focal point of the survey. The respondents exhibited a mixed view of attitudes in response towards electronic surveillance. Surprisingly, only a minority of those actually subjected to monitoring found it to be invasive or negative in any way. Other employees actually displayed positive attitudes towards high levels of surveillance in that it provided them with a deep sense of security and ensured that the line of command was set in place. In this way the results presented go against that of popular culture and the negative hype surrounding electronic surveillance. However, the authors note that a number of limitations in relation to their study, particularly in relation to sample size, restrict its generalisability and point to the need for more detailed research on this issue.

Alder *et al.,* (2006) contend that a critical task facing organisations and researchers is to identify the factors that improve employees' attitude and behavioural reactions to internet monitoring. These authors developed a causal model to explain the impact Internet monitoring has on advanced notification, justification and perceived organisational support in relation to organisational trust in the workplace. Following an initial survey, the respondents were unknowingly subjected to an Internet monitoring and filtering system implemented in their company. Afterwards they were informed that this monitoring activity was taking place. After a set time period, the sample group was sent a second survey to which only 63% of the original sample responded. When the level of employee trust and their attitude towards their specific job was examined, the results indicated that frequent users' of the Internet were more affected by the implementation of internet monitoring than those who used it on an irregular basis. Table 2 outlines literature representing employee concerns.

Table 2. Studies of Employee Dataveillance Concerns

Study	Context	Sample	Methodology
Stanton and Weiss (2000)	Identifies which attitudes, perceptions, beliefs were influenced by electronic monitoring	49 respondents from approx 25 different organisations.	Online survey
Alder *et al.,* (2006)	Examines the effects of Internet monitoring on job attitudes	62 employees from a heavy service sales and equipment sales and service centre	Two paper services were administered.

In all of the studies reviewed respondents ranged in age, location, occupation and Internet experience. For the most part the research instruments were adapted from previous studies and reused in a way specific to the study itself. A closer look at the studies presented revealed that all the researchers employed a basic survey approach administrating questionnaires and surveys to their respondents. Given the sensitive nature of the research undertaken it is not surprising to see a mixture of both paper and Web surveys utilised in the studies. For example, Alder *et al.,* (2006) opted for a traditional paper and pencil survey in their study to alleviate any concerns the employee might have in regards leaving an electronic paper trail which could be easily monitored by their employer. Similarly it may be assumed that the strict laws governing online marketing practices in Germany may in part account for the basic paper survey chosen by Singh and Hill (2003) in their study. One recurring limitation in all of the studies reviewed however appeared to be size of the samples used (Chen and Barnes, 2007; Alder *et al.,* 2006; Pavlou and Fygenson, 2006; Singh and Hill, 2003; Joines *et al.,* 2003; Stanton and Weiss, 2000). This indicates the need for an extensive and rigorous survey containing a large sample that can provide generalisable findings to progress understanding in this area.

4 Conculsion

The main aim of this paper was to provide an empirical overview of the technology-related privacy literature from both a transactional and organisational perspective. In general studies on technology-related privacy concerns are few and the construct is characterised by a lack of definitional consensus that further compounds our lack of understanding. While privacy issues have long been of concern to consumers' rights advocacy groups, the increased ability of marketers to use technology to gather, store and analyse sensitive information on consumers on a continuously updated basis has increased the acuteness of such concerns. However, the nature of such concerns and important factors that can most strongly predict or inhibit those concerns remains for the main part a matter of speculation, thus limiting our understanding of the construct.

Despite the fact that the uses of employee data surveillance technologies within organisational contexts also contain significant privacy implications, this issue has received surprisingly little attention from researchers to date. Moreover, the factors influencing employers and IS managers in their decisions to electively employ such dataveillance technologies have not been explored nor has any hierarchy of privacy concerns on the part of employers and employees been ascertained. As a result, our understanding of these issues, and the ways in which employee privacy concerns could be diminished, thus positively impacting productivity and morale, remain a matter of speculation and a fruitful avenue for researchers to explore.

5 References:

1. Acquisti, A. Protecting Privacy with Economic: Economic Incentives for Preventive Technologies in Ubiquitous Computing Environment. Workshop on Socially-informed Design of Privacy-enhancing Solutions in Ubiquitous Computing: Ubicomp (2002).
2. Acquisti, A. Privacy in Electronic Commerce and the Economics of Immediate Gratification. Proceedings of ACM Electronic Conference (EC04) New York. NY:ACM, 21--29 (2004).
3. Alder, G.S., Noel, T.W and Ambrose, M.L.: Clarifying the effects of Internet Monitoring on Job Attitudes: The Mediating Role of Employee Trust. Information and Management, (43:7), 894--903 (2006).
4. Boehle, S.: They're Watching You. Training. (37:8), 68--72 (2000).
5. Cassidy, C.M. and Chae, B.: Consumer Information Use and Misuse in Electronic Business: An Alternative to Privacy Regulation. Information Systems Management, (23:3), 75--87 (2006).
6. Chen, Y. and Barnes, S. Initial Trust and Online Buyer Behaviour. Industrial Management and Data Systems. (107:1), 21--36 (2007).
7. Cheskin eCommerce Trust Study (1999). Cheskin Research and Studio Archetype/Sapient 'eCommerce Trust Study', 1-33. Available at http://www.studioarchetype.com/cheskin/
8. Cheung, C.M.K. and Lee, M.K.O.: Trust in Internet Shopping: Instrument Development and Valiadation through Classical and Modern Approaches. Journal of Global Information Management. (9:3), July-September, 23--35 (2001)
9. Clarke, R.A. Information Technology and Dataveillance. Communication of the ACM. (31:5), 498--512 (1988).
10. Cockcroft, S. and Heales, J.: National Culture, Trust and Internet Privacy Concerns. 16th Australasian Conference on Information Systems, Sydney. (2005).
11. Concise Oxford Dictionary of Current English, Oxford University Press, England, (1996).
12. Crompton, M.: What is Privacy?. Privacy and Security in the Information Age Conference, Melbourne (2001).
13. D'Urso, S.C.: Who's Watching Us at Work? Toward a Structural-Perceptual Model of Electronic Monitoring and Surveillance in Organisations. Communication Theory. 16, 281--303 (2006).
14. Flavian, C. and Guinaliu, M. Consumer Trust, Perceived Security and Privacy Policy: Three Basic Elements of Loyalty to a Website. Industrial Management and Data Management. (106:5), 601--620 (2006).
15. Fried, C.: Privacy. Yale Law Journal. (77:1), 475--493 (1968).
16. Froomkin, A.M.: The Death of Privacy? Standford Law Review. (52:146), 1461--1543 (2000).
17. Galanxhi-Janaqi, H., and Fui-Hoon Nah, F.: U-commerce: Emerging Trends and Research Issues. Industrial Management & Data System. (104:9), 744--755 (2004).
18. Gefen, D., and Straub, D. The Relative Importance of Perceived Ease of Use in IS Adoption: A study of E-Commerce Adoption. Journal of the Association for Information Systems. (1:8) (2000).
19. Goldsmith, R. and E. Bridges.: E-Tailing versus Retailing: Using Attitudes to Predict Online Buying Behavior. Quarterly Journal of Electronic Commerce (1:3), 245--253 (2000).
20. Grabner-Krauter, S. and Kaluscha, E.: Empirical Research in Online Trust: A Review and Critical Assessment. International Journal of Human Computer Studies. (58:6), 783--812 (2003).
21. Graeff, T.R. and Harmon, S.: Collecting and Using Personal Data: Consumers' Awareness and Concerns. Journal of Consumer Marketing. (19:4), 302--318 (2002).
22. Harris Poll (2004). *Privacy and American Business Press Release* [online]. Available from: http://www.epic.org/privacy/survey/

23. Hirshleifer J. and Riley J.G.: The Analytics of Uncertainty and Information: An Expository Survey. Journal of Economic Literature. 17, 1375--1421 (1979).
24. Hoffman, D.L., Novak, T.P. and Peralta, M.: Building Consumer Trust Online. Communications of the ACM. (42:4), 80--85 (1999).
25. Hoyer, W.D and MacInnis, D.J.: Consumer Behaviour, Houghton Mifflin Company, Boston (1997).
26. Introna, L.D.: Privacy and the Computer: Why we need Privacy in the Information Society. Ethicomp e-Journal, 1. (1996).
27. Joines, J.L., Scherer, C.L. and Scheufele, D.A.: Exploring Motivations for Consumer Web Use and their Implications for E-Commerce. Journal of Consumer Marketing. (20:2), 90--108 (2003).
28. Kierkegaard, S.: Privacy in Electronic Communication- Watch Your E-Mail: Your Boss is Snooping. Computer Law and Security Report. (21:3), 226--236 (2005).
29. Konvitz, M.R.: Privacy and the Law: A Philosophical Prelude. Law and Contemporary Problems. (31:2), 272--280 (1966).
30. Kostakos, V., O'Neill, E., Little, L., & Sillence, E.: The Social Implications of Emerging Technologies. Editorial/ Interacting with Computers. 17, 475--483 (2005).
31. Lancelot Miltgen, C.: Customers' Privacy Concerns and Responses towards a Request for Personal Data on the Internet: An Experimental Study. Information Management in the Networked Economy: Issues and Solutions. 400--415 (2007).
32. Laudon, K.C. and Laudon, J.P.: Essentials of Management Information Systems: Organisation and Technology in the Networked Enterprise, Prentice Hall. 4th ed, (2001).
33. Lee, M. & Turban, E.: A Trust Model for Consumer Internet Shopping. International Journal of Electronic Commerce. (6:1), 75--91 (2001).
34. Malhotra, N.K., Kim, S.S. and Agarwal, J. Internet Users' Information Privacy Concerns (IUIPC): The Construct, the Scale, and a Casual Model. Information Systems Research. (15:4), 336--355 (2004).
35. Mayer. R. C., Davis, J.D. and Schoorman, F.D. An Integrative Model of Organisational Trust. Academy of Management Review. (20:3), 709--734 (1995).
37. Moor, J.H.: Ethics of Privacy Protection. Library Trends. 39 (1&2), 69--82 (1990).
38. Moor, J.H.: Towards a Theory of Privacy in the Information Age. Computers and Society. (27:3), 27--32 (1997).
39. Nord, G.D., McCubbins, T.F., and Horn Nord, J.: Email Monitoring in the Workplace: Privacy, Legislation, and Surveillance Software. Communications of the ACM. (49:8) 73--77 (2006).
40. Parker, R.B.: A Definition of Privacy. Rutgers Law Review. (27:1), 275 (1974).
41. Pavlou, P.A. and Fygenson, M.: Understanding and Predicting Electronic Commerce Adoption: An Extension of the Theory of Planned Behaviour. MIS Quarterly. (30:1) 115--43 (2006).
42. Platt, R.G.: Ethical and Social Implications of the Internet. The Ethicomp E-Journal, 1 (1995).
43. Powers, M.: A Cognitive Acess Definition of Privacy. Law and Philosophy. (15:4), 369--386 (1996).
44. Prakhaber P.R.: Who owns the Online Consumer? Journal of Consumer Marketing. (17:2), 158--171 (2000).
45. Ratnasinghan, P.: Trust in Web-based Electronic Commerce Security. Information Management and Computer Security, (6:4), 162--168 (1998). MCB University Press. http://www.emerald-library.com/pdfs/04606dc2.pdf.
46. Reichheld, F.F. and Schefter, P.: E-Loyality: Your Secret Weapon on the Web. Harvard Business Review. (78:4), 105--113 (2000).
47. Robey, D.: User Attitudes and Management Information System Use. Academy of Management Journal. (22:3), 527--538 (1979).

48.Rule, J.B.: Towards Strong Privacy: Values, Markets, Mechanisms, and Institutions. University of Toronto Law Journal. (54:2), 183--225 (2004).

49.Rust, R.T., Kannan, P.K. and Peng, Na.: The Customer Economics of Internet Privacy. Journal of the Academy of Marketing Science. (30:4), 455--464 (2002).

50.Safire, W.: The Great Unwatched. New York Times. (2002). Available at http://query.nytimes.com/gst/fullpage.html?res=9A03E7DB1E3FF93BA25751C0A9649C8 B63

51.Schoeman F.: Privacy: Philosophical Dimensions of the Literature: in Philosophical Dimensions of Privacy: An Anthology (F.Schoeman, ed., 1984).

52.Sheehan, K.B.: Towards a Typology of Internet Users and Online Privacy Concerns. The Information Society. 18, 21--32 (2002).

53.Singh, T. and Hill, M.E.: Consumer Privacy and the Internet in Europe: A View from Germany. Journal of Consumer Marketing. (20:7), 634--651 (2003).

54.Shih, H.: Extended Technology Acceptance Model of Internet Utilization Behaviour. Information and Management. (41:6), 719--729 (2004).

55.Smith, H.J.: Information Privacy and Marketing: What the U.S Should (and Shouldn't) Learn from Europe. California Management Review Reprint Series. (43:2), 8--33 (2001).

56.Stanton, J.M. and Weiss, E.M.: Electronic Monitoring in their Own Words: An Exploratory Study of Employees' Experiences with New Types of Surveillance. Computers in Human Behavior. (16:4), 423--440 (2000).

57.Tavani, H.T.: Internet Privacy: Some Distinctions between Internet Specific and Internet-Enhanced Privacy Concerns. The ETHICOMP E-Journal. 1, (1999).

58.Tavani, H.T.: Ethics and Technology: Ethical Issues in an Age of Information and Communication Technology. Wiley International Edition, John Wiley and Sons (2004).

59.Tracy, B.: Advanced Selling Strategies. Simon and Schuster Paperbacks, New York (1995).

60.Turban, E., Leidner, D., McClean, E., & Wetherbe, J.: Information Technology for Management – Transforming Organisations in the Digital Economy. 5th Edition. John Wiley & Sons Inc, USA (2006).

61.Udo, G.J.: Privacy and Security Concerns as Major Barriers for E-Commerce: A Survey Study. Information Management and Computer Security. (9:4), 165--174 (2001).

62.Van Slyke, C., Shim., J.T., Johnston, R. and Jiang, J.: Concern for Information Privacy and Online Consumer Purchasing. Journal for the Association of Information Systems. (7:6), 415-444 (2006).

63.Warren, S., and Brandeis, L.D.: The Right to Privacy. Harvard Law Review. (4:193), (1860).

64.Westin, A.: Privacy and F reedom. Ateneum, New York (1967).

Top Management & Enterprise Systems- The case of PPARS in the Irish Health Services

John Loonam

Dublin City University, Dublin 9, Ireland
{john.loonam@dcu.ie}

Abstract: Since the late 1990s, enterprise systems (ES) have promised to
seamlessly integrate information flowing across the organisation. They claim
to lay redundant many of the integration challenges associated with legacy
systems, bring greater competitive advantages to the firm, and assist
organisations to compete globally. These promises are timely considering the
current trends of globalisation, virtual organisations, and constant business and
technological changes, features of many strategy agendas. However, despite
such promises these systems are experiencing significant implementation
challenges. Some studies cite up to 90% failure rates. The ES literature,
particularly studies on critical success factors, point to top management support
as a fundamental prerequisite for ensuring implementation success. Yet, the
literature remains rather opaque, lacking an empirical understanding of how top
management support ES implementation. As a result, this paper seeks to
explore this theme. With a lack of empirical knowledge about the topic, a
grounded theory methodology was adopted. Such a methodology allows the
investigator to explore the topic by grounding the inquiry in raw data. The Irish
health system was taken as the organisational context, with their ES initiative
(PPARS) one of the largest enterprise systems implementations in Western
Europe. Finally, this paper will present some key observations emanating from
the emergent data.

Keywords: Top Management, Information Systems, Enterprise Systems,
Healthcare, Grounded Theory Methodology

1. Introduction

The objective of this paper is to introduce the topic of how top management support
enterprise systems, with particular interest in healthcare organisations. An initial tour
of the literature reveals a topic that has received widespread interest over the past four
decades. However, despite much discussion a lack of empirical evidence prevents
deeper understanding. Consequently, this investigation using a grounded theory
methodology seeks to build a theoretical understanding of how top management
support information systems. The case presented is that of PPARS, which is a large
SAP initiative within the Irish Health Services. This initiative commenced in 1998,
has cost in excess of €150 million, and is currently awaiting a decision with regard to
Phase III of implementation.

116

2. Nature of Enterprise Systems:

Kumar et al describe these systems as 'configurable information systems packages that integrate information and information-based processes within and across functional areas in an organisation' [1]. ESs simplify, accelerate, and automate much of the data transfers that must take place in organisations to guarantee the proper execution of operational tasks. As Davenport purports 'a good ES is a technological tour de force. At its core is a single comprehensive database. The database collects data from and feeds data into modular applications supporting virtually all of a company's business activities-across functions, across business units, across the world' [2]. Figure 1 below provides an illustration of the anatomy of an ES.

In understanding what these ES's are and what they do, Hirt and Swanson see them as "software that is designed to model and automate many of the basic processes of a company, from finance to the shop floor, with the goal of integrating information across the company and eliminating complex, expensive links between computer systems that were never meant to talk to one another" [3]. According to Nah et al, an ES is a packaged business software system that enables a company to manage the efficient and effective use of resources (materials, human resources, finance etc) by providing a total, integrated solution for the organisation's information processing needs. It supports a process-oriented view of business as well as business processes standardised across the enterprise [4]. According to Davenport (see figure 1 below), an ES package is comprised of four primary functional areas, i.e. financials, human resources, operations and logistics, and sales and marketing.

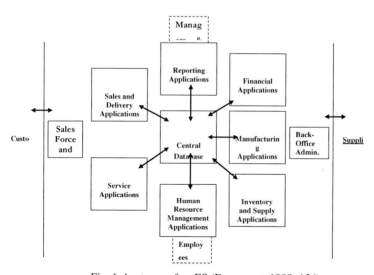

Fig. 1-Anatomy of an ES (Davenport, 1998: 124)

117

According to Stefanou, global-wide phenomena such as outsourcing, joint ventures and alliances, and partnership across the value chain, have formulated a new form of organisation described as the 'virtual enterprise'. Monolithic and stand-alone business information systems are giving way to more flexible, integrated and modular systems that support business operations across the value-chain from the supplier to the customer. [5]. Al-Mashari et al informs us that the need 'to increase visibility in corporate data, create new or improve current business processes, improve responsiveness to customers, obtain tighter integration between systems, standardise computer platforms, increase flexibility, share information globally, be Y2K compliant, and improve business performance' as reasons for the adoption of an ES [6].

The adoption of these systems is expected to bring significant benefits to the organisation. The case literature illustrates this point, with the Toro Co., saving $10 million annually due to inventory reductions, while Owens Corning claims that their ES software helped it to save $50 million in logistics, materials management, and sourcing [7]. Similarly, other cases reveal large savings in costs and increased levels of organisational effectiveness after ES implementation. Companies such as Geneva Pharmaceuticals [8], Lucent Technologies [9], Farmland Industries [10], and Digital Equipment Corporation [11], have had significant reductions in costs and increased organisational performance as a result of ES adoptions.

Yet, despite enterprise systems perceived benefits, they remain complex and expensive to implement. Kirkpatrick, for example, states that the average Fortune 500 company can spend $30 million in license fees and $200 million in consulting fees, with additional millions spent on computers and networks [12]. Similarly, the Standish Group report that 'ES implementations were on average 178% over budget, took 2.5 times longer than anticipated and delivered only 30% of the promised benefits'. Other studies report similarly poor performances. According to a survey conducted in December 2000 called "ES post implementation issues and best practices", where 117 firms across 17 countries were surveyed on their satisfaction with ES implementation projects, only 34% of the organisations were 'very satisfied' with their ES investments. Sammon et al believe that over 90% of ES implementations are late or more costly than first anticipated [13]. According to Crowe et al, further research conducted by the Standish Group International revealed that 40% of all ES installations achieved only partial implementation; nearly 28% were scrapped as total failures or never implemented, while only 25% were completed on time and within budget [14].

3. A Call for Top Management Support

Therefore, it becomes important to ask why ES implementations are delivering such poor performances, and often complete failure. Empirical investigations have focused on factors that are critical to ES success, i.e. critical success factors (CSF). In particular, top management support was identified as the most important factor for ensuring success. However, solid empirical explanations are absent from the field.

Gerald and Carroll illustrate this point in remarking that, 'a clear explanation of exactly what would constitute top management support is absent in the ES literature' [15], which is further supported by Wang et al, who noted that, 'key ES implementation factors, such as top management commitment and support….. have only been broadly discussed in the literature' [16].

Similarly, much of the IS management literature makes a continued call for greater empirical inquiry. This call, however, is as enduring as the topic itself. Garrity, for example, stated that 'top management 'must' take charge if profits are to result' [17]. A decade later Rockart and Crescenzi noted that 'in the midst of this computer-based explosion, one significant ingredient has been noticeably missing. For the most part, top management has stood-uninvolved at the sidelines. Senior executives have merely been spectators in the development and use of information systems' [18]. In the 1990s, Jarvenpaa and Ives infamously noted that 'few nostrums have been prescribed so religiously and ignored as regularly as executive support…..Despite the enthusiastic calls for executive support and the intuitively compelling evidence in the case study literature, little is known about the concept, and its utility remains largely unproven' [19]. Recently, Nathan et al, were to once again highlight the obstinate and enduring nature of this topic, remarking that 'top management support is a significant factor in influencing the effectiveness of the IS function in an organisation. The literature has conceptually supported this notion, but empirical evidence has been sparse' [20].

4. Research Methodology:

Due to the prescriptive nature of the literature, and the empirical weakness of many studies, this research used a qualitative approach known as the grounded theory method (GTM). Grounded theory method is used to develop theory that is grounded in data that are systematically gathered and analysed. The theory 'emerges' during the research process and is a product of continuous interplay between analysis and data collection (Glaser and Strauss, 1967, Strauss and Corbin, 1990). It is particularly suited to studies aiming to generate 'theories of process, sequence, and change pertaining to organisations, positions, and social interaction' [21]. GTM is also a general style of doing analysis that does not depend on particular disciplinary perspectives [22] and therefore lends itself to information systems research, which can be described as a hybrid discipline [23]. A growing body of literature attests to its range of application in IS research [24, 25, 26, 27] particularly as it is extremely useful for developing context-based, process-oriented descriptions and explanations of phenomenon [28]. Grounded theory is an inductive method of qualitative research, using a systematic set of procedures to arrive at a theory about basic social phenomenon. The method is most commonly used to generate theory where little is already known, or to provide a fresh slant on existing knowledge [29].

5. The Research Case

This study focuses on the Irish[1] Health Service. Recent large-scale public sector investment in information systems[2], a planned government programme for organisational-wide health service reform, and the ongoing implementation of Western Europe's largest ES project[3] [30] have contributed to research interest in the Irish health service. Project implementation commenced in 1998. It was decided to install a SAP R/3 system across all health boards. In the same year an 'investment appraisal' report was conducted by the DoHC. The project was endorsed as a positive move in the computerisation of the Irish Health Services. By 2000, 5 health boards had joined the project. However, implementation challenges, most notably around health board variances and the pursuit of data standardisation across all health boards, were soon to emerge. In 2001, a 'quality assessment' review of PPARS was conducted with recommendations drawing attention to a greater need for focusing on organisational issues. Consequently, Consultants were contracted in 2002 to deliver a change management programme. By 2005, DoHC concerns grew over the about of money being invested in the initiative. Consequently, further rollout of PPARS was suspended pending a 'value for money' assessment by the Irish Comptroller and Auditor General in August 2005. Phase III of the initiative is still awaiting a final decision.

The fundamental objective of an ES implementation for the health services has been born out of the desire to *integrate* its information systems. Reports talk about the pursuit of enterprise-wide [31], integrated [32], single platform [33] systems. One typical example of health service difficulties with IS disparity comes from the Southern Health Board (SHB). 'With 17,000 staff in 250 locations across Cork and Kerry, the SHB has concerns that any large enterprise can empathise with-a dispersed workforce and customers, tight budgets, and a complex communications infrastructure to manage' (CK Business Solutions, 2004). The SHB's primary concern is to integrate its dispersed IS infrastructure, allowing its agencies, customers, and staff to avail of its central information in as quick and effective manner as possible. New health reforms, e-Government initiatives, and changing health demands from citizens, now place health service providers in a unique position. The primary objective of these health reform programmes and government initiatives is to develop a people-centred, quality driven, integrated health service [34]. IS has been recognised as a dominant tool for attaining such ideals [35], where local (health board level) and national information systems can be integrated under a single platform. The primary solution to these new changes and government initiatives is the pursuit of an integrated IS strategy. The level of integration pursued by health boards, at both a local and national level, is best summed up by the north eastern health board (NEHB) who state 'IS is a major enabler that will help to deliver people-centred, quality,

---

[1] Irish refers to the Republic of Ireland only and not the Island of Ireland
[2] Referred to as information and communications technology (ICT) in the health service
[3] SAP initiative

120

integrated services….A single integrated national IS response will bring great benefits by providing comparable data across all regions' [36].

6. Some Observations:

This investigation in seeking to explore how top management support ES implementation, revealed a complex and varied topic requiring further empirical scrutiny and examination. However, while it is beyond the confines of this paper to discuss the research findings in detail, some observations will now be presented to the reader. These include;

Top managers must be aware of the magnitude and cost of IS implementation before the project begins. Implementations, such as SAP projects, are large-scale organisational initiatives requiring significant support from top management. The PPARS case reveals that decisions must be made up front with regard to project scope, budgets, and length of time required for initiative. Otherwise, such large organisational initiatives are likely to endure; sapping managerial support and organisational buy-in, whilst increasing project costs and possibly reducing project scope.

Large-scale IS implementations such as PPARS require an enterprise-wide perspective by top management. These large information systems must not be regarded as technical initiatives. Such a 'techno-centric' view, proves to be costly, with the project eventually calling for an enterprise-wide view of implementation. Consequently, the emerging data reveals that top managers must view implementation from an enterprise-wide perspective.

This study also aids in bridging the dichotomy between 'management' and 'information systems'. Many studies continued to view these two domains as separate entities. Top management support is a critical factor in the successful implementation of IS, therefore isolating both communities does little to explain the topic. Instead, greater cohesion is called for between the domains of 'management' and 'information systems', where top managers need to actively engage with IS implementation.

7. Conclusion:

This research seeks to explore top management support for the introduction of enterprise systems. A review of the literature reveals the topic has received little empirical attention over the past 40 years. This point is best summed up by Benasou and Earl, who state "as many executives have begun to suspect, the IS management traditions that have evolved over the last 40 years are flawed" (1998). The area is empirically weak and theoretically lacking. Therefore, a grounded theory method is adopted for the approach to inquiry. This approach will allow the research to build a theory grounded in data. Such a theory will not only be relevant to academia, but will also contribute significantly to top managers introducing enterprise systems into healthcare organisations.

REFERENCES

1. Kumar, K. and J. V. Hillegersberg (2000). "ERP experiences and evolution." Association for Computing Machinery. Communications of the ACM 43(4): 22-26.
2. Davenport, T. H. (1998). "Putting the Enterprise Into The Enterprise System." Harvard Business Review 76(4): 121-131.
3. Hirt, S. G. and E. B. Swanson (1999). "Adopting SAP at Siemens Power Corporation." Journal of Information Technology 14: 243 - 251.
4. Nah, F. H., J. Lee-Shang Lau and J. Kuang (2001). "Critical factors for successful implementation of enterprise systems." Business Process Management Journal 7(3): 285-296.
5. Stefanou, C. (1999). Supply Chain Management SCM and Organizational Key Factors for Successful Implementation of Enterprise Resource Planning ERP Systems. Americas Conference on Information Systems AMCIS, Milwaukee, USA.
6. Al-Mashari, M., A. Al-Mudimigh and M. Zairi (2003). "Enterprise Resource Planning: A taxonomy of critical factors." European Journal of Operational Research 146: 352-364.
7. Umble, E. J., R. Haft and M. Umble (2003). "Enterprise Resource Planning: Implementation procedures and critical success factors." European Journal of Operational Research 146: 241-257.
8. Bhattacherjee, A. (2000). "Beginning SAP R/3 implementation at Geneva Pharmaceuticals." Communications of the AIS
9. Francesconi, T. (1998). "Transforming Lucent's CFO:." Management Accounting 80(1): 22-30.
10. Jesitus, J. (1998). "Even farmers get SAPed." Industry Week 247(5): 32-36.
11. Bancroft, N., H. Seip and A. Sprengel (1998). Implementing SAP R/3: How to introduce a large system into a large organisation. Manning Publications, Greenwich, CT, USA.
12. Kirkpatrick, D. (1998). "The E-Ware War: Competition comes to enterprise software." Fortune 7: 102-112.
13. Sammon, D., F. Adam and F. Elichirigoity (2001b). ERP Dreams and Sound Business Rationale. Seventh Americas Conference on Information Systems.
14. Crowe, T. J., J. L. Zayas-Castro and S. Vanichsenee (2002). Readiness Assessment for Enterprise Resource Planning. IAMOT2002, The 11th International Conference on Management of Technology.
15. Gerald, L. and J. Carroll (2003). "The role of governance in ERP system implementation." ACIS.
16. Wang, E., H. Chou and J. Jiang (2005). "The impacts of charismatic leadership style on team cohesiveness and overall performance during ERP implementation." International Journal of Project Management 23(3).
17. Garrity, J. T. (1963). "Top management and computer profits." Harvard Business Review 41(July-August): 6-12 & 172-174.
18. Rockart, J. F. and A. D. Crescenzi (1984). "Engaging top management in information technology." Sloan Management Review 25(4): 3-16.
19. Jarvenpaa, S. L. and B. Ives (1991). "Executive involvement and participation in the management of information technology." MIS Quarterly 15(2): 205-227.
20. Nathan ?????????????????????????????
21. Glaser, B. G. and A. Strauss (1967). The discovery of grounded theory: strategies for qualitative research, Aldine de Gruyter, New York.
22. Strauss, A. L. (1987). Qualitative analysis for social scientists, Cambridge, UK: University of Cambridge Press.
23. Urquhart, C. (2000). "Strategies for Conversion and Systems Analysis in Requirements Gathering: Qualitative View of Analyst-Client Communications." The Qualitative Report 4(1/2 January).

24. Orlikowski, W. J. (1993). "CASE tools as Organisational change: Investigating incremental and radical changes in systems development." Management Information Systems Quarterly 17(3): 309-340.

25. De Vreede, G. J., N. Jones and R. Mgaya (1999). "Exploring the application and acceptance of group support systems in Africa." Journal of Management Information Systems 15(3): 197-212.

26. Howcroft, D. A. and J. Hughes (1999-April). Grounded theory: I mentioned it once but I think I got away with it. Proceedings of the UK AIS Conference, York, UK.

27. Smit, J. and A. Bryant (2000). Grounded theory method in IS research: Glaser vs. Strauss, Research in Progress Working Papers, 2000-7, 2000.

28. Myers, M. D. and D. Avison, Eds. (2002). Qualitative Research in Information Systems: A reader. London, Sage Publications Ltd.

29. Turner, B. (1983). "The use of grounded theory for the Qualitative analysis of organisational behaviour." Journal of Management Studies 20: 333-348.

30. Deloitte&Touche (2004). "Workshop Seminar." The HeBE Central Offices, Tullamore, Co. Offaly June 3.

31. DoHC (2001). "Quality and Fairness: A Health Strategy for You." Government of Ireland: 1-211.

32. DoHC (1994). "Health Strategy-Shaping a Healthier Future." Government of Ireland.

33. DoHC (2003). "Statement of Strategy: 2003-2005." Government of Ireland May: 1-48.

34. DoHC (2001). "Quality and Fairness: A Health Strategy for You." Government of Ireland: 1-211.

35. DoHC (1994). "Health Strategy-Shaping a Healthier Future." Government of Ireland.

36. DoHC (2003). "Statement of Strategy: 2003-2005." Government of Ireland May: 1-48.